THE ART OF EMPATHY

A Manual for Improving Accuracy of Interpersonal Perception

KENNETH BULLMER

*Western Michigan University
Kalamazoo, Michigan*

HUMAN SCIENCES PRESS

72 Fifth Avenue   3 Henrietta Street
NEW YORK, NY 10011 ● LONDON, WC2E 8LU

Library of Congress Catalog Number 74-11280

ISBN: 0-87705-228-X

HUMAN SCIENCES PRESS
72 Fifth Avenue
New York, New York 10011

Printed in the United States of America
89   9876543

LIBRARY OF CONGRESS CATALOGING IN PUBLICATION DATA

Bullmer, Kenneth
    The Art of Empathy.

    1. Social perceptions. 2. Interpersonal relations.
I. Title
HM132.B84   301.11   74-11280

CONTENTS

INTRODUCTION

Everyone has a need to understand other people. Much of everyone's lifetime is spent interacting with other individuals, and it is through these human relationships that people attempt to satisfy many of their own personal needs. For this reason, an individual's ability to skillfully develop and promote human relationships becomes very important.

Related intimately to people's success in developing these meaningful relationships is their ability to understand or perceive others accurately. The individual's ability to understand and predict the behaviors of others is the crucial factor in responding to other people in a way that is both appropriate to the situation and personally satisfying. It is because of this need to understand others that human beings have a tendency to form impressions of those with whom they come in contact. This tendency is an attempt to give meaning to others so that inferences concerning their personal characteristics can be made.

The process by which we form an impression or develop an understanding of another individual is that of interpersonal perception. Usually, when we form impressions of others, we respond to a great number of observable stimuli. We may take note of such diverse aspects of physical appearance as skin color, hair style, facial features and body build. The other person's actions, mannerisms, dress, vocal mode, and tone of voice may also be observed. On the basis of these cues, we usually form a rather complete idea, or percept, as to what the other person is like. But the percept that is formed is by no means limited by the available observable information; indeed, the percept will typically be completed to include inferences concerning the other person's feelings, motives, and other facets of personality.

The basis for the inferences one person makes about another is rooted in the person making the inferences. Obviously, such inferences may or may not be correct, and the degree of their accuracy will more or less determine the correctness of the percept that results from them. The individual who is generally capable of accurate interpersonal perceptions—who can perceive accurately the feelings and the meanings of those feelings of another person—is referred to here as the "Empathic Perceiver." It is this person who is in the best position to enjoy meaningful interpersonal relationships.

While a high degree of interpersonal perceptual skill is important for everyone who wants to make the most of his relationships with others, it is even more vital for those in the helping professions. In training individuals for professions involving interpersonal relations, the improvement of the trainee's interpersonal perceptual skill is generally accepted as an important factor in the effectiveness of the training. Educators in the fields of medicine, business administration, teaching, and counseling and psychotherapy have recognized that one focus of the training program should be the development of these interpersonal skills. For the professionals and the many paraprofessionals engaged in the helping process, accurate interpersonal perceptual skill becomes the *sine qua non.* Inaccuracies in percepts for these individuals strike at the very essence of their professional competence.

Although there is general agreement concerning the importance of interpersonal perceptual skill, there has been little consensus among educators over the past several decades as to how a person's ability to perceive accurately the feelings and meaning of others could be improved. Early experiments in this area proved to be very disappointing, and in time many educators came to accept that good person-perceivers were "born" rather than made. The repeated failure of clinicians in many studies to demonstrate greater accuracy of interpersonal perception than lay persons was sufficient evidence to create this subjective belief.

Perhaps as a result of this rather widely held belief and the apparent difficulty in developing and improving interpersonal perceptual skill, most training programs were developed to improve a trainee's response behaviors. They focused on developing an "empathic responder" with little attention to the development of perceptual skill.

Empathy means many things to many people, but most properly it is defined as a process whereby one person *perceives* accurately another person's feelings and the meaning of these feelings and then communicates with sensitivity this understanding to the other person. This definition makes clear the important role played by accurate interpersonal perception in the empathic process. No matter how well phrased or how sensitive a response may seem, a true state of empathy between individuals cannot exist unless the responses are based on accurate percepts. In other words, people who are considered to be highly empathic are both empathic perceivers and empathic responders.

The purpose of this book is to facilitate the development of empathic perception. The development of empathic response is left for other equally important training programs. This concentration on the improvement of interpersonal perceptual skills is intended to close a big gap in the training of professionals, paraprofessionals and lay persons. Individuals who become both empathic perceivers and empathic responders will truly be high empathizers.

Early attempts to find effective procedures for improving interpersonal perceptual skills, as stated previously, met with little success. It was this situation that prompted the research from which this book developed. An earlier edition, *Improving Your Interpersonal Perceptual Skill,* was used in a study conducted at Indiana University. Research demonstrated that subjects who learned an average of 85 per cent of the material in the book significantly improved their scores on a test of interpersonal perception. Since this original study hundreds of learners have demonstrated their ability to improve their interpersonal perceptual skills in the same manner. Average learners can be expected to improve their ability to perceive others accurately in less than eight hours of learning time without an instructor.

The book is designed so that you will learn a single principle, concept, or idea at a time. Each of the units deals with one such principle or idea. It is very important that these units be learned in the order in which they are presented. Units I and II are designed to provide background knowledge concerning the nature of interpersonal perception and the common causes of errors that occur when an individual makes inferences concerning others. This knowledge will assist you in analyzing your own perceptual skills and in determining how errors might occur and influence your perceptions of others. In addition, this knowledge will increase the significance of what you learn as a result of Units III, IV, V and VI and will thus increase the probability that your interpersonal perceptual skill will be improved.

If the procedure outlined here is followed, upon completion of this book you will be better able to understand the meaning and hidden dispositions of those with whom you are working and living and consequently be more effective in your interpersonal endeavors.

UNIT I

INTERPERSONAL PERCEPTION

The use of a word should carry with it the implication that the user knows what it means. This does not always seem to be the case, however, particularly in the case of the word "perception." Perception is a much-used word, and one that is very often used without a thought that it might be misunderstood by others.

For some individuals the term "perception" means merely visual observation. For others it means understanding or sensitivity to some person or thing, similar to empathy. Even in the field of psychology, a single, generally accepted definition of perception does not exist and, as a result, each theory of psychology has found it necessary to define the function of perception within its own system.

For our purposes as we study perception, we will view this function as a dynamic process by which a human being assigns internal meaning to the external world around him. When that which is to be perceived by an individual is another person, the function of perception involves much more than mere visual observation. In some manner the perceiver must attempt to give meaning to the other person. This process of perceiving or evaluating another person has been referred to variously as social perception, person perception, or interpersonal perception. In a sense, however, none of these terms is strictly correct, since perception proper is not what we are really dealing with. While it is true that in a sense a person is a physical stimulus not different from other physical stimuli, interpersonal perception deals *mainly* with inferences concerning the emotions, intentions, attitudes, traits and other internal properties of the perceived person. In this sense, since so many human properties are internal rather than external and cannot be observed visually, persons are not so much perceived as they are judged.

As you study Unit I, you will learn that the process of interpersonal perception, or more properly the process of one individual making inferences concerning the internal properties of another person, is influenced greatly by the perceiver's past learning experiences and thinking processes. You will also find that the process is fraught with error, since the perceiver's processes are affected by his beliefs, attitudes, values, and motives—all of which vary with individual perceivers. These beliefs, attitudes, and values may form a relatively fixed set of biases about what other people are like and how they operate and lead to serious errors in our attempts to perceive others.

There are certainly many factors that may influence your interpersonal perception, and not all of these factors will be dealt with in this manual. Special emphasis, however, is given to those factors which seem most important and most subject to control by the individual perceiver. The purpose of Unit I is to provide the basic knowledge necessary to gain an awareness of how these factors may influence your perceptions of others, but it is important that you understand that knowledge by itself is only the beginning. Gaining such an awareness involves a great amount of introspection on your part; only through introspection can you determine your implicit biases and how they.affect your interpersonal perception.

The format of this book differs from others which you may have used before. It is a programmed, self-instructional text. You will note that half of this book has been printed upside down. This has been done so that answers do not appear on a page facing the question. When you get to page 69, further instructions as to the upside-down pages will be given. Ignore these pages in the meantime.

Another difference in format is that the pages which follow are not to be read as a complete unit from top to bottom as in regular books, but should be read one item, or frame, at a time. If you turn to page 3, you will note that the items are sentences with certain words omitted. Your task is to supply the correct words where they have been omitted. As an example, the first frame to be read on page 3 is one-one. After you have read this frame and have the word in mind which you think fits, turn to the next page (page 4). In the position corresponding to item one-one on page 3, you will find the correct word (information) in the left column. In the right column of the same row you will find the next item to be read, item one-two. The correct word for item one-two will be found in the left column of the top row on page 5. In this same manner you will proceed through the text completing all the items in the top row until you are instructed to return to page 3 and begin working the second row of frames. *It is important that the frames be worked in this sequence if the material is to be meaningful.*

At the completion of each unit there is a test, so that you can check your learning of the material before beinning the next unit. Turn to page 3 now, and begin.

BEGIN HERE	**(1-1)** One definition of perception is that it is a process of extracting information from the environment. An object, a person, a condition, or any action in the environment may serve as the stimulus that activates the perceptual process of extracting _____ from the _____. Turn to page 4 now to find the correct response for this item and to read the next item.
(1-15) thinking learning	**(1-16)** Your own thinking and learning are influenced by your percepts of events, objects, and people. Also, your percepts of events, objects, and people are influenced by your _____ and _____.
(1-30) select	**(1-31)** As a result of not being able to react equally to all the stimuli available to you at one time, you may give more attention to some stimuli and ignore others. You will _____ those stimuli that will receive more attention.
(1-45) internal	**(1-46)** Interpersonal perception is an important factor in interpersonal relations. Your interpersonal perceptual skill can influence your _____ relations in many ways.

For each of the following statements, select the interpretation that seems to express best the true meaning, motives, and emotions of the person making the statement.

38. "All girls are the same. All they want is what they can get out of you."

    a. He hates all girls.

    b. He wants to know how I feel about girls and this is his way of asking.

    c. How could he really think that about girls?

    d. He's not sure how he feels about girls. His feelings are causing him a problem.

39. "I would have made a passing grade on the exam if the teacher had asked fair questions."

    a. He feels angry.

    b. He's sorry he didn't work harder.

    c. He really feels remorseful; he knows the value of studying now.

    d. He hates his teacher.

40. "I know that what I did was wrong, even though some others might have been doing the same thing."

    a. She feels ashamed of her behavior.

    b. She's rationalizing and placing the blame on others.

    c. She is experiencing guilt feelings because of her wrongdoing.

    d. She would like sympathy from me.

(1-1) information environment	(1-2) When the stimulus to be perceived by a person is another person, the process has been referred to as person perception, social perception, or interpersonal perception. We will use the term "interpersonal perception" to describe the perceptual process when the stimulus to be perceived is another person. (no response required) Turn to page 5 for the next item.
(1-16) thinking learning	(1-17) Since your percept of another person's internal properties must be based upon inferences, your inferences, as well as the percepts that result from them, will be influenced by your _____ and _____.
(1-31) select	(1-32) In a sense, a person seems to select those stimuli that will receive more _____ and those that will be _____.
(1-46) interpersonal	(1-47) We can say that interpersonal relations are influenced by the process of interpersonal perception, since the percept one person has of another will influence his response behavior toward the other person. Your percept of another individual will influence your _____ _____ toward that person.

28. When a person accepts a substitute goal that seems attainable or acceptable for a desired goal that is unconsciously seen as unattainable or unacceptable, he may be _____.

29. When someone attributes his own unconscious, undesirable feelings and motives to others, he is _____.

30. A person who perceives something that is unconsciously threatening to him may distort his perception completely to the opposite. This would be an example of _____-_____.

31. The process of ascribing to oneself qualities of another object is referred to as _____.

Identify the defense mechanism that the person making the following statements might be employing. If you think that the statement does not indicate the use of a defense mechanism, indicate this by responding "none" in the space provided.

32. _____   "Everybody will cheat if he can get away with it."

33. _____   "I devote every minute of my life to work with children."

34. _____   "I played second-string on the team this year and I felt pretty bad about it."

35. _____   "I have never had a dishonest thought in my life."

36. _____   "John has the same good traits that I have."

37. _____   "I think it's all right to cheat once in a while if it doesn't hurt anyone.

(1-2) (no response required)	(1-3) The process of one individual perceiving another individual is referred to as _____ _____. Turn to the next page for the correct response.
(1-17) thinking learning	(1-18) Stated simply, your past learning and your thinking processes will _____ the manner in which you make _____ about the internal properties of other individuals and the _____ that you will form concerning these other individuals.
(1-32) attention ignored	(1-33) Since you must respond selectively to the many stimuli available, you must somehow determine which stimuli you will deal with. Factors that will influence your selection of stimuli for attention are your past _____ and your _____ processes.
(1-47) response behavior	(1-48) In other words, your response behavior toward another person is dependent upon your _____ of the other person. Also, the other person's _____ _____ toward you will be dependent upon his _____ of you.

17. Since one cannot perceive all available stimuli simultaneously when attempting to perceive another person, the perceptual process must be s_____.

18. The "common sense" set of notions that people have about what other people are like and how they operate has been referred to as their _____ _____ _____.

19. When you assume that another's values and traits are the same as your own, you may be using _____ similarity as your basis for the inference.

20. It is probably fair to say that human beings are always in some state of _____ that produces motives which lead to behavior.

21. Anxiety is always an _____ feeling.

22. It is not easy to avoid e_____ the statements of others when our own strong e_____ are involved.

23. Anxiety that is controlled by responses and does not manifest itself in overt behavior is referred to as controlled, or _____, anxiety.

24. Psychologists refer to the noninstrumental responses that an individual may employ to distort reality as _____ _____.

25. A person who finds his usual method of attaining a goal blocked and then seeks out a new method of attaining the same goal is employing an i_____ response to reduce anxiety caused by the situation.

26. Human needs and _____ and _____ are closely related.

27. When a person gives a plausible reason for behavior that is motivated by unconscious, unacceptable impulses, the mechanism being employed is referred to as _____.

(1-3) interpersonal perception	(1-4) Many theorists, however, suggest that persons are not so much perceived as they are known and judged, since many human properties are internal rather than external. While external properties can be observed visually, one individual cannot observe the _____ properties of another person.
(1-18) influence or effect inferences percepts	(1-19) Since no two persons have exactly the same learning experiences or thinking processes, perception should be viewed as an individual process. A stimulus may result in one percept for one person while the same stimulus may result in an entirely different _____ for another person.
(1-33) learning thinking	(1-34) It is this selection process, influenced by the perceiver's unique learning experiences and thinking processes, which accounts for the differing percepts of the same person by two different perceivers. It is as if each perceiver _____ different stimuli for attention and then deals with them in his own unique manner.
(1-48) percept response behavior percept	(1-49) Your use of implicit personality theory, your thinking, your sets, and your motives may influence your interpersonal perception determining your _____ _____ toward other persons.

7. Three major causes of inaccurate inferences concerning another person are inadequate i_____, d_____, and the use of _____ _____ _____.

8. Someone who thinks that all children are bad is said to be _____.

9. Verbal statements can be interpreted from the viewpoint of the v_____ c_____ of the statement or from the viewpoint of the _____ _____ of the statement.

10. According to the _____ approach to understanding the meaning of the other person, behavior must be perceived from the other person's _____ of _____.

11. It seems that we often have a tendency to _____ what is said by the other person.

12. If you wanted to improve your ability to perceive others accurately, you would benefit from the procedures of _____-_____.

13. Three behavioral manifestations of implicit personality theory are s_____, assumed _____, and _____ attribution.

14. You will improve your ability to infer accurately the meaning of others when you learn to interpret their statements from the viewpoint of the _____ intent of their statements.

15. One of the major sources of inaccurate perceptions of others is _____ of stimuli; this serves as a buffer against realities with which the perceiver is unable to cope.

16. A technique for avoiding the natural tendency to evaluate has been referred to as _____ with _____.

(1-4) internal	(1-5) Interpersonal perception is a process by which one in-dividual perceives the external properties *and* the _____ properties of another individual.
(1-19) percept	(1-20) Others may have similar but not exactly the same past learning experiences and thinking processes as you. Consequently, your _____ will differ to some degree from those of others.
(1-34) selects	(1-35) Two persons having different percepts of the same person at the same time cannot both be accurate to the same degree. Just as past learning and thinking processes contribute to accuracy of percepts, so does the _____ of stimuli to which the per-ceiver is responding.
(1-49) response behavior	(1-50) If appropriate response behaviors are important for you, it would seem then that you would benefit from gaining an awareness of the factors that are influenc-ing your response behaviors. Most importantly, you would want to make explicit your _____ _____ theory.

Final Proficiency Test

This test provides the final opportunity for you to evaluate what you have learned from this course of study. The test is somewhat longer than previous ones, since it is designed to test your understanding of all the preceding material, as well as that in Unit VI. If you have worked through all six units and learned the material in such a way that you now understand the concepts and ideas that were presented, you should experience little difficulty in providing appropriate responses for the following items. On the other hand, if your efforts to learn the material have been directed primarily toward merely memorizing the terms used and the examples, you may experience a good deal of difficulty with this test. If this should be the case, these items will then serve as a guide to your review of Unit VI and the previous units where appropriate.

When you have completed all items in the test, turn to the answer key and check your responses against those in the key.

Supply the missing words in the following statements:

1. Many factors that influence a person's perceptions have their basis in the perceiver's _____.

2. Some of the important factors that influence a person's perceptions are p_____ l_____, _____ processes, mental "____," and m_____.

3. The process by which one individual becomes aware of the properties of another individual is referred to as _____ _____.

4. Not all properties of the stimulus person can be easily observed visually since many properties are _____.

5. The meaning, motives, and emotions of human beings can be inferred accurately by interpreting the person's appearance, motor behavior, and _____ behavior.

6. The process of perceiving another human being is complicated and has many sources of _____.

(1-5) internal	(1-6) When one person attempts to perceive another person, the external properties of the person to be perceived are easily observed visually, but other means must be found to perceive that person's _____ properties.
(1-20) percepts	(1-21) If your past learning experiences and your thinking processes were different from what they are, your percepts of people would probably be somewhat _____ from what they are now.
(1-35) selection	(1-36) Your past learning and thinking processes as well as your selection of stimuli for attention will influence the _____ of your percepts.
(1-50) implicit personality	(1-51) Understanding your own behavior is not easy, however, since much of the time your ways of behaving are habitual and you are hardly aware of what you are doing. As a result, it is difficult for you to gain an awareness of your own _____ _____ _____ without your making a special effort to do so.

(6-72)	(6-73)
C	"I wouldn't want his car and money if somebody gave them to me."
The emotion of guilt is a feeling of wrongdoing. The key here is her feeling of having done wrong.	A. He may be envious and he would like those things.
	B. He is a real down-to-earth kind of guy.
	C. He's trying to make me feel sorry for him.
	D. He feels angry.

Return to page 130 for the next item.

(1-6) internal	**(1-7)** A person's internal properties such as emotions, motives, attitudes, and abilities cannot generally be observed visually by another person. If they are to be known, these _____ properties of an individual must be inferred.
(1-21) different	**(1-22)** The greater the difference between your past learning experiences and thinking processes and those of another person, the more you might expect that your percepts will be _____ from those of that other person.
(1-36) accuracy	**(1-37)** Other factors involved in determining which stimuli are responded to and which are ignored are the perceiver's "set," and the perceiver's motives in play at the time. As well as past learning and thinking, _____ and _____ of the perceiver may influence his percepts.
(1-51) implicit personality theory	**(1-52)** If you are to work toward improving your ability to perceive others, you must somehow begin with the process of self-analysis so that you can gain an awareness of your own implicit personality theory and the ways in which it may affect your interpersonal _____ skill. The process of _____-_____ can lead to this awareness for you.

(6-71)

D

This fits the classic pattern of jealousy—the loved one giving attention to someone else who is perceived as a rival. Anger and anguish are components of jealousy and, therefore, B and C may also apply.

(6-72)

"I know that I should not have cheated, even though the others were doing it."

A. She is rationalizing and trying to put the blame on the others.

B. She cheated and should pay for it.

C. She feels guilt because she thinks that cheating is wrong.

D. She really doesn't feel very bad.

(6-77)

C

Remember not to evaluate. See if you can perceive the world as he perceives it, even if he appears to stereotype you.

END OF UNIT VI

Turn to page 136 for the final proficiency test.

(1-7) internal	(1-8) If one individual is to know the traits and intentions of another individual, these internal properties of the other person must be _____.
(1-22) different	(1-23) Therefore, we can see that interpersonal perception is an individual process that can vary among individuals even when they are dealing with the same _____ at the same time.
(1-37) set motives	(1-38) When we attempt to perceive another human being, we almost always do it with a motive. This motive may influence our _____ of that human being.
(1-52) perceptual self-analysis	(1-53) One procedure for gaining an awareness of the conceptual framework from which you operate is _____-_____.

(6-70)

B

Anger generally results from the blocking of goal-attainment. This produces frustration and anger is likely to follow when a source can be identified.

(6-71)

"She broke our date so she could spend the weekend showing her friend around town."

A. He should forget her.

B. He feels sorry for himself.

C. He is angry because she broke the date.

D. He is jealous of the attention that she gave to her friend.

(6-76)

D

This is an example of possible rationalization. She may not be able to accept that she feels it is wrong to engage in premarital sex.

(6-77)

"All teachers are the same. They don't give a damn about students."

A. He hates all teachers.

B. He is trying to make me angry.

C. Teachers are a source of anxiety for him in some way.

D. He doesn't really think that. How could he?

(1-8) inferred	(1-9) Our original definition of perception was that it was a _____ of extracting _____ from the environment.
(1-23) person or individual	(1-24) Interpersonal perception becomes much more compli-cated than object perception since we can use visual perceptual processes to perceive objects, but must _____ the internal characteristics of hu-man beings.
(1-38) percept	(1-39) When we have expectations of perceiving certain things or events, or have a "set," it is possible that our percept will be influenced by our _____.
(1-53) self-analysis	(1-54) One step in the procedure of self-analysis involves making your beliefs about others, or your implicit personality theory, explicit. You must know what these beliefs are if you are to understand how they might affect your interpersonal perception. This is the first step in improving your _____ _____ skill.

(6-69)

A

If you didn't select A, you have gone overboard and you are interpreting beyond what is there. This is dangerous, so be on guard against it.

(6-70)

"I would have completed my paper on time if my roommate hadn't walked off with my notes."

A. She could have borrowed some notes.

B. She is angry because of her roommate.

C. She is feeling guilt because she didn't complete her paper.

D. She must have a very bad roommate.

(6-75)

B

If you selected A, C, or D, you are reading too much into this statement. Do not look for meaning that is not there.

(6-76)

"There is nothing wrong with premarital sex because it's a biological instinct."

A. It *is* an instinct and I admire her for admitting that it is.

B. She's committing a sin.

C. She feels happy with her behavior.

D. She may be anxious about her sexual behavior.

(1-9)	(1-10)
process information	In interpersonal perception, where the stimulus is another person, you must extract or perceive _____ about the person to be perceived.
(1-24) infer	(1-25) One important factor that contributes to making interpersonal perception more difficult than object perception is that a person is at the same time a physical stimulus and more than a physical stimulus. The physical stimulus, or external properties, of a person may be viewed as visually observable, but the _____ properties of a person are not observable and must be _____ .
(1-39) set	(1-40) As well as past learning and thinking processes, our _____ and our _____ can also influence our percept of another person.
(1-54) interpersonal perceptual	(1-55) It is important that professionals such as teachers, social workers, counselors, and clinicians develop their ability to perceive others accurately. Inaccurate perceptions on the part of the professional strike at the very essence of his professional competence. The process of _____-_____ will be a beginning toward improving your ability to perceive others.

(6-68)

A

Fear is a strong emotion. The key point here is the feeling of being powerless to avoid the threat.

(6-69)

"There were eight children in our family —four boys and four girls."

A. There were four boys and four girls in his family.

B. He doesn't like his brothers and sisters.

C. He likes being part of a large family.

D. He's angry because his parents had so many children.

(6-74)

D

The longer the striving, the greater is the joy when we attain our goal.

(6-75)

"The engine in my car needs repairs and I need 250 dollars."

A. He wants to ask me for money.

B. The engine needs repair and he needs money for it.

C. He feels remorseful because he doesn't like to spend money.

D. He is angry because of the engine.

(1-10) information	(1-11) If the information extracted from the stimulus person is not accurate, it can be expected that the percept, or what is perceived, will also not be _____.
(1-25) internal inferred	(1-26) The real object of interpersonal perception is perceiving the essence and attributes of the person to be perceived. These are internal properties that are not physical and, therefore, not directly _____.
(1-40) set motives	(1-41) As a result of past learning, each of us has developed certain attitudes, beliefs, and values. These contribute to a relatively fixed set of biases for each of us about what other people are like. This set of biases has been referred to as the "implicit personality theory" of the perceiver and it influences a person's _____ of another person.
(1-55) self-analysis	END OF UNIT I Turn to page 18 and complete the proficiency test to determine your mastery of the ideas and concepts presented in Unit I.

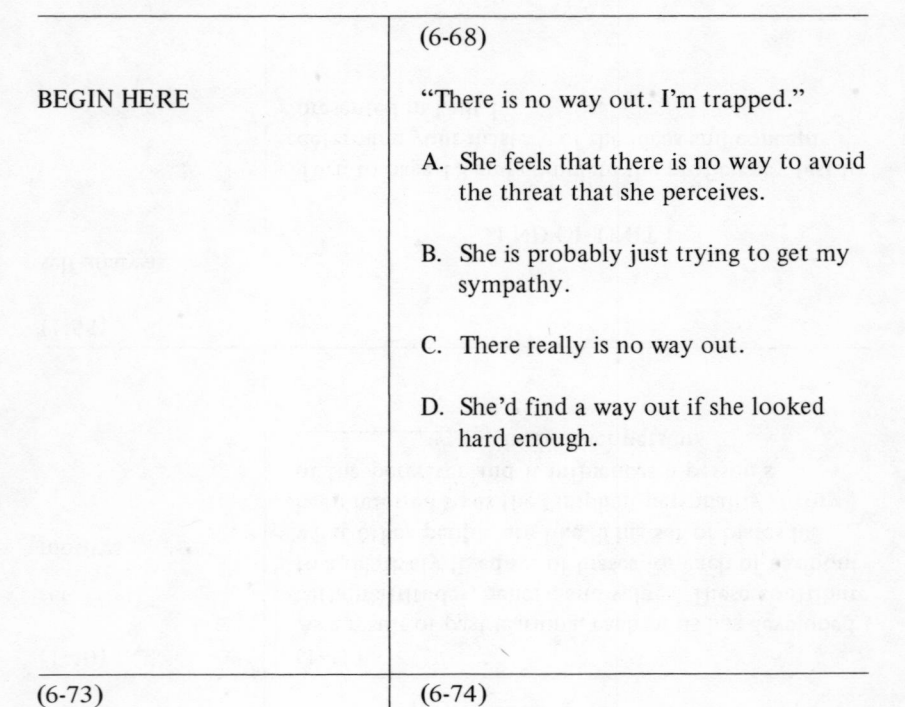

BEGIN HERE

(6-68)

"There is no way out. I'm trapped."

A. She feels that there is no way to avoid the threat that she perceives.

B. She is probably just trying to get my sympathy.

C. There really is no way out.

D. She'd find a way out if she looked hard enough.

(6-73)

A

First he feels envious, but this feeling is perceived as being bad, and this makes him feel anxious. Result: reaction-formation.

(6-74)

"I can hardly believe that I have it. I've waited for it for a long time."

A. She is angry that it took so long.

B. She has it now.

C. She wants to impress me.

D. She is experiencing a state of joy.

(1-11)

accurate

(1-12)

In other words, a person's percept of another person is related to the information extracted or perceived from the stimulus person. The accuracy of a person's percept of another person can vary depending upon the _____ of the information perceived.

(1-26)

observable

(1-27)

If these internal properties of another person are to be known by a perceiver, they must be inferred. The appearance, motor behavior, and verbal behavior of the person to be perceived provide the basis for _____ his internal properties.

(1-41)

percept

(1-42)

Without realizing it, the perceiver has a "built-in" theory about what other people are like, and this theory may influence his percepts and judgments about other people. This theory, or "common sense" notion of what other people are like and how they operate, has been referred to as the perceiver's _____

_____   _____.

Section 2: Final Practice

This section has been designed to give you a final opportunity for practicing the technique of listening with understanding. Each of the following items contains a statement and several possible interpretations of the statement. Your task is to select the interpretation that reflects most appropriately the possible affective intent of the statement. Remember, avoid the tendency to evaluate the statement from your frame of reference by first trying to restate the expression in such a way that it could reflect the possible frame of reference of the person making the statement.

Turn to page 130 now and begin with item 6-68.

(1-12)	(1-13)
accuracy	Our original definition of perception stated that it was a process. It can be viewed as a dynamic _____ with interdependent parts.
(1-27)	(1-28)
inferring	Another factor that can complicate interpersonal perception is that the perceived person may withhold certain stimuli information from the perceiver. In this situation, it becomes more difficult for the perceiver to make accurate _____ about the internal properties of the stimulus person.
(1-42)	(1-43)
implicit personality theory	The use of your implicit personality theory, or common sense notions, may provide the basis for your selection of stimuli from the many provided by the stimulus person and in this manner have an important influence on your percept of that person and the degree of _____ of that percept.

(6-17)

implicit
personality
theory

error

(6-18)
An individual is said to be stereotyping when he attributes identical characteristics to any member of a class or group regardless of the actual degree of variation within the class. The notion that all members of a racial group have low intelligence is an example of _____ and it leads to _____ in interpersonal perception.

Return to page 111 for the next item.

(6-35)

frame

reference

(6-36)
In addition, after we _____ the other person's statement, we often have a tendency to make a judgment and approve or disapprove the statement.

Return to page 111 for the next item.

(6-53)

infer

(6-54)
It is sometimes the case that the other person is not willing or able to express his real emotional state through either bodily reactions or verbal expressions. Consciously or unconsciously the other person may attempt to conceal his true _____.

Return to page 111 for the next item.

(1-13) process	(1-14) These interdependent parts are learning and thinking, and they are parts of the total dynamic perceptual _____.
(1-28) inferences	(1-29) In interpersonal perception, it is important that the perceiver understand that the stimulus person may be withholding certain stimulus information and/or that he may not be presenting cues that can be accepted at face value as indications of his true _____ properties.
(1-43) accuracy	(1-44) A person's attempts to perceive the internal properties of another person may be influenced not only by his set, motives, and thinking processes, but also by his use of _____ _____ _____ that has resulted from his past learning experiences.

(6-16)	(6-17)
implicit personality theory	Implicit personality theory, which is also a personality factor, is expressed through perceptual behavior; specifically, through the use of stereotyping, trait attribution, and assumed similarity. These three behavioral manifestations of _____ _____ _____ can contribute to _____ in interpersonal perception.
(6-34)	(6-35)
frame	It is a difficult task to view things from the other person's frame of reference because of our natural tendency to evaluate the verbal content of the statement from our own _____ of _____.
reference	
(6-52)	(6-53)
emotional	Emotional states are also characterized by verbal reactions. It is, therefore, possible to identify some emotional states by interpreting accurately the verbal expressions of an individual. If you can accurately interpret an individual's verbal statement, you can then accurately _____ his emotional state.

(1-14) process	(1-15) In other words, perception can be viewed as a dynamic process that influences and is influenced by its interdependent parts. These interdependent parts are _____ and _____ . Return to page 3 for the next item.
(1-29) internal	(1-30) Under most conditions there are many more things to be perceived about a person than can possibly be perceived simultaneously. As a result of this perceptual limitation, the perceptual process must be selective. In other words, the perceiver must _____ the stimuli to which he will respond. Return to page 3 for the next item.
(1-44) implicit personality theory	(1-45) Two different perceivers, each perceiving the same stimulus person at the same time but having different implicit personality theory as well as different motives, sets, and thinking processes, could very possibly infer different _____ properties of the stimulus person. Return to page 3 for the next item.

(6-15) distortion error	(6-16) The use of implicit personality theory is another major source of error in interpersonal perception. As a result of our past learning and thinking processes, each of us has developed certain beliefs, attitudes, and values that contribute to a relatively fixed set of biases about how people are and how they operate. It is this set of biases that are referred to as the perceiver's _____ _____ _____ .
(6-33) affective intent	(6-34) Sometimes, you must be able to identify hidden meaning, motives, and emotions of the stimulus person if you are to infer accurately his f_____ of r_____ .
(6-51) emotions motives	(6-52) Emotional states are often characterized by facial and other bodily reactions. It is, therefore, possible to identify some emotional states by observing changes in facial expressions and other bodily reactions such as gestures and to infer the _____ state of the stimulus person.

Proficiency Test for Unit I

The purpose of this proficiency test is to enable you to determine your mastery of the concepts and ideas presented in Unit I. This test is planned as a learning experience for you, rather than as a "testing" experience. If it is used with that purpose in mind, it should serve to reinforce what you have already learned as well as to point out any parts of the unit that may need additional review before proceeding to Unit II.

The following items differ from the ones you have just completed in that the correct responses are not given to you immediately after you complete an item. The strategy here is for you to supply the missing words for all items by writing them in the spaces provided. When you have responded to all items, check your responses by turning to the answer key for Unit I at the end of the text. If you find that you have encountered difficulty with certain items, you should return to Unit I and review the material dealing with those items until you feel certain that you have a complete understanding of the material. When you are satisfied in this respect, you are then ready to proceed to Unit II.

1. Perception has been defined here as a process of extracting _____

   from the _____.

2. Perception is a dynamic _____ with interdependent parts. These interdependent parts are _____ and _____.

3. It has been suggested that persons are not so much perceived, as they are known and judged, since many human properties are _____ and cannot be observed visually.

4. People have a "common sense" set of notions about what people are like and how they operate. This set of notions is referred to as their _____

   _____ _____.

5. Since there are usually many more things to be noticed about a stimulus person than you can possibly perceive simultaneously, your perceptual process must be _____.

6. Two factors that may influence your perceptual process are your expectations, or "____," and your _____.

(6-14) distortion error	(6-15) When the perceiver, as a result of his past learning, thinking, mental set, or motives, perceives a threat to his existing perceptual organizations, _____ of stimuli is most likely to occur and lead to _____ in his perceptions.
(6-32) verbal content affective intent	(6-33) Your ability to infer accurately the stimulus person's frame of reference will be improved considerably when you have developed skill at interpreting verbal expressions from the viewpoint of the _____ _____ of the statement.
(6-50) emotions	(6-51) Emotional states are associated with some of the same internal responses to needs as are motives. For this reason, it is generally accepted that there is a close relationship between _____ and _____.

7. Gaining awareness of your own internal properties may involve the procedure of _____-_____.

8. Your faulty percept of another person may result in inappropriate
   _____ behavior by you toward that person.

9. Since internal properties of an individual cannot easily be observed by another individual, they must be _____ if they are to be known.

10. Perception should be viewed as an individual process since no two persons
    have the same past _____ _____ or _____ processes.

11. Your interpersonal perceptual skill can influence your _____
    relations.

12. Your percept of another person may vary in degree of accuracy depend-
    ing upon the degree of _____ of your inferences concerning that
    person's internal properties.

(6-13) distortion	(6-14) The past learning, thinking, mental set, and motives of the perceiver are personality factors that influence his perceptions and can be the basis for _____ of stimuli and _____ in his interpersonal perceptions.
(6-31) verbal behavior	(6-32) Verbal behavior can be interpreted from two different viewpoints. It can be interpreted from the viewpoint of the verbal content, or the literal meaning of the words, or from the viewpoint of the affective intent. Affective intent refers to the feeling, or emotion, that is being expressed. Two viewpoints from which the statements of others can be interpreted are _____ _____ and _____ _____.
(6-49) behavior	(6-50) Emotion, as a human experience, refers to an individual's subjective feelings of pleasantness or unpleasantness. Anger, fear, happiness, and anxiety are common words that describe pleasant or unpleasant subjective feelings or _____.
(6-67) improving your interpersonal perceptual skills requires constant *practice*	END OF SECTION 1 Turn to page 129 and begin Section 2.

UNIT II

SOURCES OF ERROR
IN INTERPERSONAL PERCEPTION

In Unit I we examined how individuals go about perceiving other individuals, or the process of interpersonal perception. The perceiver's past learning, thought processes, set, and motives were identified as factors that influenced the perceptual process.

In Unit II we shall examine some of the characteristics of the good person-perceiver and some of the common sources of error in interpersonal perception. Analysis of these perceiver characteristics and the common sources of error will make it possible to identify three major sources of error in interpersonal perception—errors caused by inadequate intelligence, errors caused by distortion, and errors caused by the use of implicit personality theory.

The objective of Unit II is for you to gain an understanding of the ways in which distortion and the use of implicit personality theory by the perceiver can result in errors in interpersonal perception.

The design of the Unit II format is the same as it is for Unit I, and you should proceed in the same manner as when you read Unit I, reading by frames rather than by pages. As in Unit I, a test is provided so that you can check your learning at the completion of the unit.

Turn to page 21 and begin with the first frame, 2-1.

(6-12) greater (or high) lesser (or low)	(6-13) Distortion of stimuli involves falsifying, modifying, or denying the existence of stimuli so that what is perceived is not accurate. Personality factors of the perceiver are the basis for _____ of stimuli.
(6-30) frame reference	(6-31) Your ability to infer accurately the other person's frame of reference is enhanced considerably when you are skilled at interpreting his verbal behavior. It is possible to identify the meaning, motives, and emotions of others by interpretation of their _____ _____.
(6-48) satisfaction	(6-49) It is probably reasonable to believe that the human being is always in some state of need, and, therefore, the human being always has motives that produce _____ of some kind, which has as its purpose the satisfaction of needs.
(6-66) affective intent infer	(6-67) It is not easy to enter into the perceptual world of another person. Practicing the technique of listening with understanding and interpreting verbalizations so as to be able to infer accurately their affective intent will be a big step toward developing this ability. When you have learned to do this, you should find that your interpersonal perceptual skills are improved. Remember, _____ _____ _____ _____ _____ _____ _____ _____.

BEGIN HERE	**(2-1)** There are many sources of error in interpersonal perception. Superficial observation, faulty memory, erroneous premises, mistaken inferences, superstitions, prejudice, and perceptual distortion of stimuli are some of the many _____ of _____ in interpersonal perception.
(2-10) greater or high intelligence	**(2-11)** The perceiver's use of _____ _____ theory has also been identified as a major source of error in interpersonal perception.
(2-20) implicit personality theory error	**(2-21)** Another way in which the use of implicit personality theory contributes to error in interpersonal perception is its use by the perceiver to attribute related traits to apparent traits. "Big men are brave," and "Red hair indicates a quick temper," are examples of the use of implicit personality theory in attributing _____ traits to apparent _____.
(2-30 implicit personality theory stereotyping trait attribution	**(2-31)** In summary there are *three* major sources of error in interpersonal perception. One major source of error involves the _____ of stimuli by the perceiver.

(6-11)	(6-12)
sources error interpersonal	Intelligence, which is a personality factor, is related to the perceiver's ability to organize incoming stimulus material into meaningful and useful configurations. Persons with _____ intelligence are able to manage this function with greater effectiveness than are persons with _____ intelligence.
(6-29) sources error	(6-30) One way of guarding against errors that result from the tendency to distort stimuli and the use of implicit personality theory is by using the perceptual approach to understanding the other person. This involves perceiving things from the stimulus person's frame of reference rather than from your own _____ of _____.
(6-47) motive	(6-48) Motives usually lead to some behavior the purpose of which is the _____ of needs.
(6-65) verbal content	(6-66) Again, you must learn to listen with understanding—to interpret the verbalization and infer the _____ _____ of the other person's statement rather than evaluate the verbal content of the statement from your frame of reference. If you are able to do this, you will be able to _____ accurately the meaning, motives, and emotions of the other person.

(2-1) sources error	(2-2) Analysis of these various sources of error suggests *three major* classifications: errors caused by distortion, errors caused by inadequate intelligence, and errors caused by the use of implicit personality theory. Thus, three _____ sources of error can be identified.
(2-11) implicit personality	(2-12) When somebody has formed a fairly definite impression of another person (feels that he is warm and friendly or cold and hostile) for reasons he is unable to spell out, he is probably making use of his _____ _____ _____ to form his impression of the other person. This practice may be a source of _____ in interpersonal perception.
(2-21) related traits	(2-22) Trait attribution is a behavioral manifestation of the perceiver's _____ _____ _____, and may lead to _____ in interpersonal perception.
(2-31) distortion	(2-32) Another major source of error in interpersonal perception is inadequate _____. We can expect that persons with greater _____ will be more accurate in perceiving others than will persons who have lesser _____.

(6-10) personality	(6-11) Three major sources of error can be identified, all of which have their basis in the perceiver's personality. These are inadequate intelligence, perceptual distortion, and the use of implicit personality theory. These are three major _____ of _____ in _____ perception.
(6-28) interpersonal perceptual self-analysis	(6-29) The second step in your attempts to improve your interpersonal perceptual skills—your ability to infer accurately the meaning, motives, and emotions of others—should be directed toward finding ways to overcome the major _____ of _____ in your interpersonal perceptual process.
(6-46) learned needs	(6-47) Needs produce internal responses that psychologists call motives. The purpose of motives is the satisfaction of needs. A person who is experiencing a hunger need usually has a _____ to find food.
(6-64) reaction-formation	(6-65) Thus, if you are to identify accurately emotional states of anxiety in others by interpreting their verbalizations, you must be prepared to interpret the hidden meaning behind their statements. The true meaning of persons who are employing defense mechanisms to control anxiety will not be evident from the _____ _____ of their statements.

(2-2) major	(2-3) The three major sources of error in interpersonal perception are errors caused by _____, errors caused by inadequate _____, and errors caused by the use of _____ _____ _____.
(2-12) implicit personality theory error	(2-13) One way in which we see the use of implicit personality theory contributing to error in interpersonal perception is its use by the perceiver to close gaps in his knowledge about others. People seem to have a tendency to close gaps in their knowledge about others so as to be able to perceive the complete person. The use of _____ _____ _____ in this process of attempting to perceive the whole person can be a source of _____ in interpersonal perception.
(2-22) implicit personality theory error	(2-23) In trait attribution the perceiver assumes that the presence of one trait necessarily follows from the presence of another _____.
(2-32) intelligence intelligence intelligence	(2-33) The third major source of error in interpersonal perception is the tendency of perceivers to employ their _____ _____ _____ as it is expressed through _____, trait _____, and assumed _____.

(6-9) error	(6-10) Since an individual's perceptions are influenced by his personality, the major sources of error in interpersonal perception can be viewed as having their basis in the perceiver's own _____.
(6-27) accurate	(6-28) Gaining awareness of your personality and how it affects your perceptions of others is the first step toward improving your i_____ p_____ skills. You can gain this awareness through the procedure of _____-_____.
(6-45) biological needs	(6-46) Another way of categorizing needs is as learned needs. Prestige, achievement, and money are some examples of _____ _____.
(6-63) projection	(6-64) Reaction-formation involves preventing desires that are perceived as threatening from being expressed by exaggerating the opposite attitude. A person who desires something that is threatening for him may distort this desire completely to the opposite and claim that he has never desired that thing. This would be an example of _____-_____.

(2-3) distortion intelligence implicit personality theory	(2-4) Each percept is unique to the person who is experiencing it. When we consider perceptual distortion, we are really considering individual differences in perception. Different percepts formed by different perceivers of the same stimulus can be accounted for by perceptual _____.
(2-13) implicit personality theory error	(2-14) First impressions and snap judgments based on implicit personality theory may result from the perceiver's attempt to close the gaps in his knowledge about another person. Stated differently, the perceiver's desire to close gaps in his knowledge about another person may lead to first _____ and snap _____ based on implicit personality theory and may lead to _____ in interpersonal perception.
(2-23) trait	(2-24) Trait attribution is a process of assigning characteristics to a person. It is a process of inferring inner dispositions from observable actions and characteristics. When we infer that somebody is insensitive because he uses coarse language, this process is referred to as _____ _____ because we have inferred an internal characteristic from observable actions.
(2-33) implicit personality theory stereotyping attribution similarity	(2-34) Because implicit personality theory is not subject to objective verification, its use by teachers, counselors, social workers, or clinicians inhibits seriously their professional effectiveness. Its use by lay persons as well as professionals may result in _____ in their interpersonal perceptions and affect their response behaviors and their interpersonal _____.

(6-8) behavior	(6-9) The process of interpersonal perception, or inferring the meaning, motives, and emotions of a stimulus person is very complicated, and there are many sources of _____ in the process.
(6-26) internal	(6-27) A person who unknowingly distorts stimuli and makes use of implicit personality theory cannot be aware that his perceptions may not be _____.
(6-44) needs	(6-45) Needs can be categorized in different ways. One such category would be biological needs. Food, water, air, and sleep are some examples of _____ _____.
(6-62) identifying	(6-63) When someone attributes his own undesirable, unconscious feelings and motives to others, he is projecting. In a sense, identification can be viewed as the opposite of _____.

(2-4)	(2-5)
distortion	In Unit I you learned that set and motives influenced your perceptual processes by determining which stimuli would be attended to and which stimuli would be ignored. This selective function in the interpersonal perceptual process is one way in which perceptual _____ occurs.
(2-14) impressions judgments error	(2-15) Implicit personality theory is expressed through perceptual behavior; specifically through the use of stereotyping, trait attribution, and assumed similarity. These three behavioral manifestations of _____ _____ _____ may contribute to _____ in interpersonal perception.
(2-24) trait attribution	(2-25) In the process of trait attribution, related traits are inferred from apparent traits. When a perceiver infers internal characteristics of another person from the physical appearance of that person, we say that he is employing _____ _____. This is a behavioral manifestations of _____ _____ _____ and may lead to _____ in interpersonal perception.
(2-34) error relations	(2-35) Someone who is attempting to improve his interpersonal perceptual skills will benefit from the procedure of self-analysis. Self-analysis enables him to gain awareness of his _____ beliefs and thus make them explicit. These beliefs are then subject to objective _____.

(6-7) inferred	(6-8) Internal human properties can be inferred from the appearance, motor behavior, and verbal behavior of the stimulus person. It is possible to infer accurately the meaning, motives, and emotions of the stimulus person by interpreting accurately his verbal _____ .
(6-25) self-analysis	(6-26) By becoming more aware of the personality factors that influence your perceptions—your past learning, thinking processes, beliefs, attitudes, and values—you can better understand and cope with your tendencies to make inaccurate inferences concerning the _____ properties of other persons.
(6-43) needs motives	(6-44) All human beings have needs. Such things as food, water, achievement, and money are examples of human _____ .
(6-61) compensating	(6-62) Ascribing to oneself qualities and characteristics of another person or object is referred to as identification. The person who acts as if he shared in the traits and characteristics of someone else may be _____ with that person.

(2-5)	(2-6)
distortion	Perceptual distortion may occur as a result of the _____ of stimuli to be attended to or ignored by the perceiver.

(2-15)	(2-16)
implicit personality theory errors	Three behavioral manifestations of a perceiver's implicit personality theory are his use of _____, _____ attribution, and assumed _____.

(2-25)	(2-26)
trait attribution implicit personality theory error	If you were to infer that a person was an athlete and had a low I.Q. for no other reason than that he had a powerful physique and a low forehead, you would be using the process of _____ _____ because you would be inferring _____ traits from the _____ traits.

(2-35)	(2-36)
implicit verification	You must know what your beliefs about others are if you are to understand your use of _____, trait _____, and _____ similarity.

(6-6) internal	**(6-7)** If the internal properties of the stimulus person are to be known by the perceiver, their existence must be _____, since they cannot be observed visually.
(6-24) personality	**(6-25)** If a person is to understand his own tendencies to make errors in his interpersonal perceptions, it would seem that he would profit from the procedure of self-analysis. Attempting to become aware of our own personality factors is involved in the procedure of _____-_____.
(6-42) affective intent emotions	**(6-43)** Human emotions are closely related to needs and mo- tives. If you are to have an understanding of emotions, therefore, you must also have an understanding of _____ and _____.
(6-60) rationalizing	**(6-61)** Accepting a substitute goal that seems attainable or socially acceptable for a desired goal that is perceived as unattainable or socially unacceptable is an example of compensation. Someone who avoids an activity in which he cannot excel and concentrates on another activity in which he can excel may be _____.

(2-6) selection	(2-7) Perceptual distortion can occur because what is perceived must fit the needs of the perceiver. The perceiver's needs direct his _____ of stimuli to be attended to or ignored and it is this process that may lead to perceptual _____.
(2-16) stereotyping trait similarity	(2-17) An individual is said to be stereotyping when he attributes identical characteristics to any member of a class or group, regardless of the actual degree of variation within the class. The notions that members of certain racial groups have more or less intelligence are examples of _____.
(2-26) trait attribution related apparent	(2-27) In trait attribution the perceiver tends to place emphasis on the extremes or traits that he values highly. If the perceiver values intelligence he tends then to rate others as either having _____ intelligence or low _____ rather than differentiating along the total continuum of intelligence.
(2-36) stereotyping attribution assumed	(2-37) The procedure of _____-_____ would enable you to gain awareness of your implicit beliefs about other people so that you may improve your _____ _____ skills.

(6-5) interpersonal perception	(6-6) Interpersonal perception is far more complicated than is object perception, since many of the properties of the stimulus person are _____ and cannot be observed visually.
(6-23) stereotyping trait attribution assumed similarity	(6-24) All of these sources of error have their basis in the perceiver's own _____.
(6-41) natural evaluate	(6-42) It is possible to become skilled at this technique, how-ever, by practicing the interpretation of verbal expres-sions and by having knowledge about human emo-tions. If you are to interpret verbal expressions from the viewpoint of the _____ _____ of the statement, it is prerequisite that you have an un-derstanding of human _____, which are the basis for these statements.
(6-59) defense mechanisms	(6-60) The defense mechanism by which a person gives plau-sible reasons for behavior that is motivated by uncon-scious, socially unacceptable impulses is referred to as rationalization. The person who says, "It's OK to cheat on exams, because everybody does it," may be _____.

(2-7)	(2-8)
selection distortion	Perceptual distortion may result when a perceiver feels threatened and feels the need to defend his existing perceptual organizations. The perceiver's capacity to confront life openly and without undue defensiveness contributes to his *accuracy* in perceiving others by lessening the perceiver's need for distorting the attributes of the stimulus person. Undue defensiveness impairs _____ in perceiving others and increases the need for perceptual _____.
(2-17) stereotyping	(2-18) When we engage in a brief conversation with an older person we have never met before, and for reasons we cannot spell out, we feel that he has little respect for us, we may be _____ this person. This is a behavioral manifestation of our _____ _____ _____.
(2-27) high intelligence	(2-28) Assumed similarity is a process whereby a perceiver attributes to other persons characteristics that he sees himself as possessing. A person who sees himself as trustworthy may assume that others are trustworthy. In such a case, he is using the process of _____ _____ to infer the disposition of the other person. This is a behavioral manifestation of _____ _____ _____.
(2-37) self-analysis interpersonal perceptual	(2-38) Since the perceiver's tendency to distort stimuli to fit his own needs and goals can only be accounted for in terms of the perceiver's personality, the procedure of _____-_____ would help the perceiver to reduce errors in his interpersonal perception.

(6-4) learning thinking set motives	(6-5) When the stimulus to be perceived is another person, the process is referred to as _____ _____. This is the process by which one human being perceives another human being.
(6-22) intelligence distortion implicit personality theory	(6-23) The ways in which implicit personality theory is expressed in behavior are _____, _____ _____, and _____ _____.
(6-40) before evaluate	(6-41) It is difficult to learn to listen with understanding—to interpret the affective intent of the other person's statement—rather than evaluate the verbal content of the statement since it seems to be a _____ tendency to _____.
(6-58) noninstrumental	(6-59) Rationalization, compensation, identification, projection, and reaction-formation are terms that identify some of the _____ _____ that people employ to distort, falsify, or deny stimuli in an effort to reduce anxiety.

(2-8) accuracy distortion	(2-9) "Beauty is in the eye of the beholder" is an old proverb that emphasizes the ability of the perceiver to select stimuli so that he can perceive what he chooses to perceive. A perceiver who has a need to perceive beauty may _____ stimuli to be attended to which will fit his need and by so doing, the _____ of his percept may be influenced.
(2-18) stereotyping implicit personality theory	(2-19) The sets of biases employed in stereotyping seem to be unaffected by the situation itself. The same sets and biases appear to operate regardless of differences in the situation. When you find that you are stereotyping, you are employing sets of _____ that are not affected by the situation.
(2-28) assumed similarity implicit personality theory	(2-29) In cases of assumed similarity, the perceived person is not viewed as being different from the perceiver in certain essential and meaningful ways. In its most extreme form, _____ _____ involves exact correspondence between the values, motives, and goals of the perceiver and those of the perceived. This process may lead to serious _____ in the perceiver's percept of the other person.
(2-38) self-analysis	 ### END OF UNIT II Turn to page 31 for a proficiency test to determine your mastery of material presented in Unit II.

(6-3) different percepts	(6-4) The perceptual worlds of different persons differ because of differences in the factors that influence their percepts. Each person's percepts are influenced by his own personality—his past _____, _____ processes, mental "_____," and m_____.
(6-21) assumed similarity error	(6-22) In summary, the three major sources of error in interpersonal perception are inadequate _____, perceptual _____, and the use of _____ _____ _____.
(6-39) listening understanding	(6-40) A way to facilitate listening with understanding and avoiding the tendency to evaluate is to restate the other person's statement so that it reflects the affective intent *before* you respond to the statement. It is important that this be done _____ you respond to the statement if you are to avoid the natural tendency to _____ the statement.
(6-57) instrumental	(6-58) If that same person seeks to distort, falsify, or deny the existence of his desired goal, he is employing a _____ response, or a *defense mechanism*.

(2-9) select accuracy	(2-10) Incoming stimulus material is organized into configurations that are useful and meaningful to the perceiver. The perceiver's ability to manage this intellectual function well, or to perceive accurately, is closely related to the perceiver's intelligence. We can assume that persons with _____ intelligence will be more accurate in their perceptions than will those with lesser _____. Return to page 21 for the next item.
(2-19) biases	(2-20) Stereotyping is an example of a behavioral manifestation of _____ _____ _____ and it may lead to _____ in interpersonal perception. Return to page 21 for the next item.
(2-29) assumed similarity error	(2-30) The use of assumed similarity is one behavioral manifestation of _____ _____ _____. Two others are _____ and _____ _____. Return to page 21 for the next item.

(6-2) perceive differently	(6-3) Each individual's perceptual world is _____ from the perceptual worlds of others because each in- dividual's perceptual world is influenced by his own unique psychological state: his percepts are a reflec- tion of his *personality*—his sensory abilities, cognitive capacity, experience, motives, values, and other traits. As individual personalities differ, so do individual _____, which are a reflection of personalities.
(6-20) trait attribution error	(6-21) Assumed similarity is a process whereby a perceiver attributes to other persons characteristics that he sees himself as possessing. When a perceiver sees *exact* cor- respondence between his values, motives, and emo- tions and those of the stimulus person, it is an extreme form of _____ _____, and it can lead to _____ in interpersonal perception.
(6-38) affective intent	(6-39) One technique that can help you to avoid the tenden- cy to evaluate, judge, and approve or disapprove the statement of the other person has been referred to as "listening with understanding." It is possible to inter- pret accurately the other person's frame of reference —the affective intent of his statement—by employing the technique of _____ with _____.
(6-56) instrumental noninstrumental	(6-57) Instrumental responses reduce anxiety by eliminating the causative conflict or frustration. As an example, a person who is frustrated because he cannot achieve his goal one way, and then seeks out a new way to reach his goal and relieve his frustration, is employing an _____ response to reduce frustration.

Proficiency Test for Unit II

The purpose of this test is to provide an opportunity for you to determine your understanding of the material presented in Unit II before you go on to the next unit. The procedure to be followed for this test is the same as with the test for Unit I. Supply the missing words for each item, and when you have completed all items, check your responses with those in the answer key at the end of the text. If you find that your responses do not correspond with those in the answer key, return to the text and review the material until you are sure that you understand all of Unit II.

1. Implicit personality theory is expressed through perceptual behavior by

   the use of _____, _____ _____, and

   _____ _____.

2. When a person infers _____ traits from apparent traits, the process is

   referred to as _____ _____.

3. Gaining awareness of your own personality through the procedure of

   _____-_____ can be helpful in reducing error in your interpersonal

   perception.

4. If you want to improve your interpersonal perceptual skills, you will bene-

   fit from making your _____ _____ _____ explicit

   so that it can be examined and tested.

5. Careful analysis of the many causes of error in interpersonal perception

   suggests that three major sources of error can be identified. There are er-

   rors caused by perceptual _____, errors caused by inadequate

   _____, and errors caused by the use of _____

   _____ _____.

6. Someone who assumes that another's motivation is the same as his own

   motivation is said to be using _____ _____ as his basis for

   perceiving the other person.

(6-1) process information environment	(6-2) Each individual lives within his own unique perceptual world. In other words, the world for him is as he perceives it to be, and in many ways it can be different from the perceptual worlds of other individuals. For this reason, different individuals can _____ the same object or person _____.
(6-19) stereotyping	(6-20) Trait attribution is a process of assigning characteristics to a person. It is a process of inferring dispositions of the stimulus person from observable actions and characteristics. When we infer that someone has low intelligence because he doesn't do well in school, we are imploying _____ _____, and it can be a source of _____ in interpersonal perception.
(6-37) evaluate judgment approve disapprove	(6-38) Somehow, rather than evaluate the other person's statement on a basis of how you perceive the world, you must interpret the statement on a basis of the other person's meaning, motives, and emotions. You must go beyond the verbal content of the statement and interpret the a_____ i_____ of the statement.
(6-55) anxiety	(6-56) You should recall that motives produce behavior, and the behavior that is produced to lessen anxiety can be of two kinds: instrumental responses or noninstrumental responses. Anxiety can be reduced by means of either _____ or _____ responses.

7. Someone who attributes identical characteristics to all teachers is said to be _____.

8. The selective function in the interpersonal perceptual process is one way by which perceptual _____ may occur.

9. Incoming stimulus material is ordered and organized into cognitive configurations that are meaningful to the perceiver. The perceiver's ability to manage this function well is closely related to high _____.

10. The perceiver's rather well-developed "common sense" notions of what other people are like and how they operate is referred to as the perceiver's _____ _____ _____.

BEGIN HERE	**(6-1)** Perception can be viewed as the process by which a human being becomes aware of the stimuli in his environment. It is the _____ of extracting _____ from his _____.
(6-18) stereotyping error	**(6-19)** The notions that all Republicans are conservative and that all Democrats are liberal are other examples of _____.
(6-36) evaluate	**(6-37)** If you are to interpret the other person's statement from the viewpoint of the affective intent of the statement, i.e., from the other person's frame of reference, you must avoid the tendency to _____ the statement, make a _____, and _____ or _____ the statement.
(6-54) emotions	**(6-55)** Anxiety is an unpleasant emotional state, and usually a person who is experiencing anxiety will attempt to reduce the degree of unpleasantness. The person's need is for the more pleasant state created by removing the source of the _____.

UNIT III

IDENTIFYING EMOTIONS

Section 1: Needs, Desires, Motives, and Emotions

If you are to employ explicit theories and ideas that are concerned with the identification of another person's meaning, a prerequisite to this ability is an understanding of the concepts of needs, desires, motives, and emotions. A need can be defined as a person's compulsory feeling to remove or change his perception of physiological or psychological discomfort or disturbances within himself. These feelings of discomfort or disturbance may be stomach pangs signaling a need for food or drink, or they may have to do with the individual's relationship to his environment. The person who perceives himself to be in danger of physical harm may experience a need to avoid danger. Often, a person perceives disturbances in his relations with other individuals—he may perceive himself as being disliked and ignored or as being dominated by others —and as a result, he feels a need to change the situation in some way.

Need states produce internal responses that psychologists call drive states or motives. These motives usually result in some overt behavior in which the individual attempts to influence his environment in such a way so as to alter his need state. In addition to feelings of discomfort, desires are also a source of motives and behavior. Unlike needs, however, desires are not feelings of discomfort but are feelings of wish or urge toward certain objects, persons, or activities. These objects, persons, or activities are perceived as pleasure-producing. In other words, motives produced by needs are directed toward avoiding discomfort, while motives produced by desires are directed toward producing pleasure. Both kinds of motives produce goal-directed behavior.

Emotion usually refers to an individual's subjective feelings that are associated with the same internal responses as are motives. For this reason, both emotions and motives are closely related to each other and are both associated with human needs. Although it has been customary in psychology to distinguish between motives and emotions, these two concepts have such a close relationship that many contemporary theorists now view motives and emotions as two slightly differing viewpoints from which to regard the same behavior. As an example, the person who is experiencing the emotion of anxiety may be motivated to seek relief. The relationship between the emotion

33

UNIT VI

SUMMARY

By now you have learned that your perceptions define the meaning of the other person for you. You have also learned that there are several factors involved in interpersonal perception that can lead to inaccuracies in your perceptions. Perceptual accuracy becomes the *sine qua non* for teachers, counselors, clinical psychologists, social workers, and everyone who is called upon to make appropriate professional responses to other persons. For this reason, then, you have practiced using some techniques that should prove helpful in your attempts to understand the meaning, motives, and emotions of other individuals. At this point, you should have an understanding of the pitfalls you must guard against as well as some ideas as to how to go about doing a better job of perceiving the meaning of others.

The purpose of Unit VI, the last in this course of study, is to review in summary form what you have already learned from the previous units and to provide additional practice in perceiving accurately the meaning of others by interpreting the affective intent of their verbalizations. This should be an opportunity for you to "put it all together" and to make clear any points that you do not understand fully at this time. A test is provided at the end of the unit so that you can make an evaluation of your learning.

Turn to page 111 now and begin with Section 1.

and the motive in this example is such that it becomes difficult to distinguish between them.

Now turn to page 35 and begin with item 3-1. As in the previous units, you are to work rows of frames by turning the page after reading an item.

7. "I don't think it's wrong to want things for yourself."

   a. She doesn't care how I feel about her.

   b. She is selfish and doesn't think of others.

   c. She doesn't feel bad about thinking of herself.

8. "I get angry at times, but so does everybody else."

   a. He may be having difficulty accepting his feelings of anger.

   b. He has a bad habit of getting angry.

   c. He thinks it's OK to get angry because others do it.

9. "I'm really a terrible person."

   a. She has done something bad.

   b. She is feeling remorseful about her behavior.

   c. She wants me to see her as a bad person.

10. "My parents treat me very badly, but I love them very much."

   a. He doesn't mind that his parents treat him that way.

   b. He'd love his parents no matter what they did to him.

   c. He is confused about his feelings and may not really love his parents.

11. "Nobody can help me."

   a. She feels this is something she is obligated to do on her own.

   b. The thought of talking about it is making her very anxious.

   c. She feels that it is too late for help.

BEGIN HERE	**(3-1)** A person's most significant experiences occur in relation to the satisfaction of his needs. Without needs there might well be no behavior or significant experiences for the individual. For this reason, behavior of another person can be interpreted as an attempt to satisfy some _____.
(3-8) biological	**(3-9)** In the course of his development from infancy to adulthood, the human develops various _____ needs that serve to _____ his behavior.
(3-16) emotion motives	**(3-17)** Motives are accompanied by the experience of emotion which also can serve to _____ behavior.
(3-24) verbal content	**(3-25)** Vocal mode of speech and _____ _____ are both important for communicating emotions and can be used as a basis for inferring the _____ states of others.

Proficiency Test for Unit V

This test will provide an opportunity for you to check your understanding of the perceptual approach to perceiving meaning in others and to see how skillful you are at identifying the meaning of others by listening with understanding to their statements.

In this test you will find some statements that are missing words, as well as some multiple choice questions. Again, you can write your answers in the space provided and, when you have completed the test, you can check your answers against those in the answer key at the rear of the text.

Supply the missing words in the following statements:

1. Understanding the meaning of the other person by perceiving things from his frame of reference rather than from your own frame of reference has been referred to as the _____ _____.

2. It seems that we have a natural tendency to _____ the statements made by other persons from our own _____ of _____.

3. You are likely either to approve or disapprove the other person's statement after you have made a _____ about the statement.

4. It is not easy to avoid evaluating the statements made by others when strong _____ of your own are involved.

5. A way to overcome the tendency to evaluate the statements of others is by _____ with _____. This requires a great deal of _____ if you are to become proficient at doing it.

For each of the following statements, select the response that seems to express most appropriately the ideas and feelings of the person making the statement.

6. "I can't stand hippies."

   a. He doesn't know how he feels about hippies.

   b. Hippies make him feel angry.

   c. He thinks hippies are less than human.

(3-1) need	(3-2) Needs can be categorized in different ways. One such category would be biological needs. Food, water, air, proper temperature, sleep, and sex are some examples of _____ needs.
(3-9) learned motivate	(3-10) The adult human being has both _____ needs and _____ needs.
(3-17) motivate	(3-18) As an example, the person who is experiencing the emotion of anger may be _____ to strike out at the cause of his anger.
(3-25) verbal content emotional	(3-26) In addition to identifying emotions by accurately interpreting expressive reactions such as facial changes and other bodily reactions, you can also identify emotions by interpreting verbal statements. Inferences concerning another person's emotions can be made on the basis of his verbal statements. Both _____ mode of speech and verbal _____ are important means of communicating emotion.

(5-36)

B or D

If you selected B, you are probably correct. The self-directed aggression is possibly the result of her frustration.

(5-37)

"Studying is a needless waste of time."

A. He doesn't feel there is any value in education.

B. He's just lazy and doesn't want to do any work.

C. He is concerned about his ability to handle his school work.

D. He would like me to argue the point.

Return to page 100 for the next item.

(3-2) biological	(3-3) Needs can also be categorized as learned needs. Prestige, achievement, and money are examples of _____ needs.
(3-10) biological learned	(3-11) Learned motives, which result from learned needs, may be stronger than those that are produced by _____ needs.
(3-18) motivated	(3-19) Just as internal reactions are characteristic of emotional states, external reactions are also characteristic. Facial and other bodily reactions are examples of _____ reactions that can be observed during emotional states.
(3-26) vocal content	(3-27) You will have improved your interpersonal perceptual skill considerably when you have learned to _____ accurately the _____ states of others by interpretation of their verbal statements.

(5-35)

A

It could be B or D if you have reason to interpret her statement as a defense against anxiety and a distortion of reality.

(5-36)

"I could just beat myself for getting into this jam."

A. She feels she is a pretty bad sort of person to be in this position.

B. She feels a good deal of aggression.

C. She shouldn't have allowed herself to get in this position.

D. She feels frustrated.

(5-43)

D

You'll be right with this choice most of the time. Remember that all people have needs that they attempt to satisfy in what seems to them to be the best way.

END OF UNIT V

If you think you have the idea at this point, turn to page 108 and complete the test for Unit V. If you have any doubts, review the practice items before moving on to the test.

(3-3) learned	(3-4) Needs produce internal responses that psychologists term drive states or *motives,* the purpose of which is the satisfaction of needs. Thus, needs lead to motives which in turn usually lead to behavior by the individual. Behavior of others can then be interpreted as an attempt to satisfy some _____ and as being directed by a _____ .
(3-11) biological	(3-12) A person who refuses food when hungry in order to be polite probably has stronger _____ needs than he has _____ needs.
(3-19) external	(3-20) Changes of facial expression can be characteristic of emotional reactions. Smiling, laughing, and crying behaviors are indicative of_____ .
(3-27) infer emotional	**END OF SECTION 1** Turn to page 43 and begin Section 2.

(5-34)

C

If you selected D, you may be correct. He is rigid and demonstrates it by stereo-typing. That is his defense against conflict and anxiety.

(5-35)

"I know that there is a way and I'll find it."

A. She feels pretty hopeful!

B. She's rationalizing because there is no way out.

C. She's overly confident in her abilities to handle this situation.

D. She doesn't want me to know how hopeless she feels.

(5-42)

B

It would make you feel good if A and C were true, but B seems more appropriate. D might be true, but there is no reason to make this judgment unless you have something else to go on—your emotions or hers.

(5-43)

"I have only one goal in life—to be of ser-vice to others. I really don't want any-thing for myself."

A. He doesn't want or receive anything.

B. He must be stupid to feel that way.

C. He thinks he's better than I am.

D. He really does want something for himself.

(3-4) need motive	(3-5) Motivation usually leads to some behavior the purpose of which is the satisfaction of some _____.
(3-12) learned biological	(3-13) Emotion, as a human experience, usually refers to an individual's subjective feelings of pleasantness or un-pleasantness. Anger, fear, happiness, and sorrow are common words that describe different kinds of _____.
(3-20) emotions	(3-21) Emotions can, therefore, be inferred from observable expressive reactions such as changes in facial expression and other bodily reactions such as nervousness, gestures, and changes in voice tone. When you observe that a person is smiling or frowning, you can make an inference concerning his _____ state.

(5-33)

D

Anxiety is the emotion again. If you selected A, you're being somewhat defensive yourself. If you selected B, you may be on the right track, but it seems likely that it would be rationalization.

(5-34)

"All counselors are the same. You think alike."

A. He really likes counselors or he wouldn't be here.

B. He feels all counselors think alike.

C. He's afraid that I will not understand what he is going to say.

D. He's pretty damn rigid.

(5-41)

A

How's that for an example of stereotyping and perhaps assumed similarity! What defense mechanism might she be employing to control her anxiety?

(5-42)

"There is nobody who can help me but you."

A. She knows I'm the only person who can solve her problems.

B. She feels very dependent upon my providing her with answers.

C. She realizes that I have special skill in solving problems.

D. She thinks she can seduce me this way.

(3-5) need	(3-6) When motivated behavior is successful, it reduces the need state and thus the _____ for behavior.
(3-13) emotions	(3-14) Emotional states are also associated with internal responses. Internal reactions such as changes in blood pressure, heart rate, and sweating are distinctive characteristics of _____ states.
(3-21) emotional	(3-22) Another of man's ways of expressing or communicating emotional states is by speech. Normal human speech is one of the most prominent means of expressing emotions. A person's verbal behavior is a basis for making inferences concerning his emotions. *Vocal mode* of speech and the *verbal content* are two aspects of verbal behavior that are important to consider when you are making inferences concerning a person's _____.

(5-32)

D

He may be dealing with his anxiety by means of non-instrumental responses. In that case, D represents the emotion that leads to A, B, and C as responses to control the anxiety.

(5-33)

"I really don't think you can help me."

A. She thinks I'm not capable.

B. She feels that nobody could help her and she must think it out alone.

C. Her condition is such that she is beyond help.

D. She feels anxious and talking about it is somewhat threatening to her.

(5-40)

A

You should recognize the frustration. Since an instrumental response was not possible, it is likely that she tried a noninstrumental response. The result would be rationalization.

(5-41)

"All people are the same. They are just out to get you."

A. She is afraid that she is inadequate in some way.

B. She feels that people are born bad and stay that way.

C. She feels that I'm bad.

D. She doesn't like people and she doesn't need them.

(3-6) motive	(3-7) It is probably reasonable to believe that the human organism is always in some state of need. This means that the human is always motivated toward some form of _____.
(3-14) emotional	(3-15) You have already learned that motivation is also associated with some of the same internal respons-es as is emotion. For this reason, _____ and _____ are generally viewed as being very inti-mately related.
(3-22) emotions	(3-23) The vocal mode of speech is important for communi-cation of emotional states. The manner in which a phrase such as "I am happy" is spoken determines to a large degree the emotional state that is being ex-pressed. Emotions can then be inferred from the _____ _____ of speech.

(5-31)

C

Look for the emotion—in his case, fear. Again, A, B, and D are good examples of evaluating, judging, and approving the statement.

(5-32)

"Young people should be free to make their own decisions at age 16. They should be free to vote and do as they please."

A. He feels adolescents are mature and should vote.

B. He feels proud that he is free.

C. He feels hatred.

D. He feels anxious about authority.

(5-39)

C

A is not very likely to be the case if he is a human being with needs. B might be true, but it is still probably a defensive response. If you selected D, you might ask yourself why you feel this way.

(5-40)

"As bad as the situation was, there was nothing I could do to change it."

A. She felt frustrated because of her inability to do anything about it.

B. She felt it was impossible and did the right thing.

C. She knew what the outcome would be.

D. It was an impossible situation and nobody could deal with it differently.

(3-7)	(3-8)
behavior	The newborn infant has not acquired learned needs. The newborn infant begins life with only _____ needs.
	Return to page 35 for the next item.

(3-15)	(3-16)
emotion	In other words, needs lead to internal responses that can lead to both _____ and _____.
motives	
	Return to page 35 for the next item.

(3-23)	(3-24)
vocal mode	Although vocal mode of speech is important for communicating emotions, the verbal content of the statement "I am happy" also communicates the existing emotional state. Emotions can be inferred from the vocal mode and also from the _____ _____ of the statement.
	Return to page 35 for the next item.

(5-30)

B

There are lots of opportunities here for you to evaluate, and if you selected A as your choice, you are also judging and approving.

(5-31)

"I think we should drop a hundred atom bombs on Russia and wipe them out."

A. He really hates Russians.

B. He's some kind of a screwball who likes war.

C. He is afraid that Russia will drop an atom bomb on his home some day.

D. He's pragmatic and pragmatism has its value.

(5-38)

A

This seems to be a case of identification and displacement. The aggression is directed toward someone less threatening than the person it is really meant for.

(5-39)

"I don't let anything bother me."

A. He doesn't get anxious about anything.

B. He feels he's pretty cool.

C. He feels it's difficult to cope with conflicting emotions.

D. He feels I couldn't cope with things that bother him.

Section 2: Description of Specific Emotions

In a sense, classifying specific emotions would seem to be an impossible task. Emotions occur as one aspect of a specific experience for an individual and, because of the infinite variety of human experiences, there is an infinite variety of human emotions. Each emotional experience is unique to the individual who is experiencing it. However, even though each emotional experience such as "fear," for example, differs to some extent from every other experience of "fear," all of these experiences of fear do seem to have some common characteristics. This is true also for other forms of emotional experience and on this basis, it seems reasonable to establish characteristics that are common to specific emotions.

As you have already learned, emotions are evoked by the physiological and psychological state of a person. Since needs, desires, and motives are closely related to emotions, our attempts to describe an emotion should take place in relation to its situational determinants. As you analyze specific emotions in this section, it should become clear that each emotion is characterized by certain kinds of situations that play a part in determining that emotional experience.

The range of human emotions is vast and no attempt will be made here to describe all emotions that human beings might possibly experience. Rather, several of the more common emotions will be dealt with, and the essential situational conditions and common features of these specific emotions will be described.

Turn to page 44 now and begin with item 3-29. When you complete this section, you should know the situational conditions that are commonly related to certain emotions and the essential features of these feelings.

BEGIN HERE

(5-30)

"I hate school and all my teachers."

A. He thinks school is pretty bad and I'm inclined to agree.

B. He is extremely unhappy with his school situation for some reason.

C. He is not very ambitious and doesn't care about an education.

D. He feels unhappy because he has bad teachers.

(5-37)

C

At this point, you should have had no difficulty in selecting C as the appropriate response.

(5-38)

"I don't know for sure what you've done, but I'd still like to smack you one."

A. He sees something in me that makes him feel aggressive.

B. He hates me.

C. He suspects I've done something to him that he doesn't know about.

D. He thinks everybody is hostile and that makes him aggressive.

BEGIN HERE	**(3-29)** Fear is an emotion that accompanies the perception of a dangerous or threatening situation. Since there are many potentially threatening situations in everybody's environment, _____ is a common emotional experience.
(3-35) joy	**(3-36)** The intensity of the emotion of joy will depend upon the importance of the goal, the difficulty encountered in attaining it, and the suddenness with which the goal is attained. An important goal that is attained after long striving may produce intense _____. Remember, the intensity of the emotion of joy will depend on the _____ of the goal, the _____ encountered in attaining it, and the suddenness with which the goal is attained.
(3-42) success	**(3-43)** If the quality of his performance falls short of his expected level of achievement, he may see this as "bad" and he may have feelings of _____.
(3-49) shame guilt	**(3-50)** Many emotions are directed toward other people. Love, hate, jealousy, and envy are emotions that have as their situational basis a person's relations to other _____.

Section 2: Practice

It has been suggested that the best way to learn to listen with understanding is to practice doing it. One method of practicing is for you to delay responding to another person until you have first restated the ideas and emotions that were expressed. By doing this, you will be forced to see things as the other person is seeing them, and your natural tendency to evaluate the other person's statement will most likely be thwarted.

This is something that you can work on in your everyday encounters with other people. You may expect that the more you practice, the more your interpersonal perceptual skills will improve.

To help you get the idea, the sequence of items on the following pages is designed so that you can first read a statement and then attempt to restate it to yourself, reflecting the emotions that may have provoked the statement. After you have done this, you will find several restatements that could reflect the emotions of the person making the statement. Your strategy should be to select the restatement that seems to express most appropriately the possible emotions and ideas of the person making the statement.

Turn to page 100 now and begin with item 5-30. See if you can interpret the statements from the other person's frame of reference—from his unique perceptual world.

(3-29) fear	(3-30) The essential characteristic of fear is the perception of a dangerous or _____ situation. Fear is a common _____ experience.
(3-36) joy importance difficulty	(3-37) Anger is an emotion that can also be associated with goal-attainment. When an individual is blocked in his attempts to attain a goal, and he can identify the object or person preventing his goal-attainment, _____ is likely to occur.
(3-43) failure	(3-44) Pride and shame are deeper emotions than are feelings of success and failure. When the accomplishments or lack of accomplishments are perceived by an individual as reflecting his basic qualities, he may experience _____ as a result of his success and _____ as a consequence of his failure.
(3-50) people	(3-51) The emotion of love may take many different forms depending upon how a person perceives his relationship with the other person. The essential characteristic of love, however, seems to be that the person is drawn to the other person and desires to be drawn to the other person. A feeling of devotion to the loved person is also a characteristic of _____.

(5-7) emotions	(5-8) An example of this would be somebody saying "There isn't a God" to somebody who is deeply religious. The first response we might expect to such a statement would be to _____ the statement. The religious person might then think "That is not true," which is _____ the statement. He might also make a _____ about the person making the statement. Return to page 91 for the next item.
(5-15) perceives different	(5-16) The first step in perceiving things from the other person's frame of reference is to avoid the natural tendency to _____ the other person's statement from your frame of reference and then _____ the statement, approving or disapproving it. Return to page 91 for the next item.
(5-23) risk	(5-24) It requires a great deal of courage to risk entering the perceptual world of someone who is expressing ideas that you strongly disagree with. In these cases, it is doubly difficult to listen with understanding, since it not only requires courage to _____ possible change on your part, but your own _____ are strongly involved. Return to page 91 for the next item.

(3-30) threatening emotional	(3-31) An important factor in the situation leading to fear is the perception of being unable to avoid the threat. When a person perceives a threat and is unable to see a way of avoiding it, _____ may result.
(3-37) anger	(3-38) An essential feature of the situation producing anger is that the person can identify the obstacle to his goal. When a person cannot identify the obstacle to his goal, _____ is not as likely to occur as when he can identify the cause of his not being able to attain his goal.
(3-44) pride shame	(3-45) In other words, a person who perceives *himself* as "good" because his behavior meets his expectations may experience the emotion of _____ and a person who perceives *himself* as "bad" because his behavior does not meet his expectations may feel _____.
(3-51) love	(3-52) The emotion of hate is not merely dislike of another person. Hate involves an intense feeling of dislike to the extent that there is a desire to destroy the hated person or object. When a person dislikes another person, his tendency is to avoid that person, but with hatred, the tendency is to seek out the hated person and _____ him.

(5-6) evaluation	(5-7) Our tendency to respond to statements in this manner seems to be related to the involvement of our own emotions. Our tendency to evaluate, judge, and approve or disapprove the statements of others is increased when our own _____ are strongly involved.
(5-14) percept percepts	(5-15) If you are to understand the meaning of the other person, you must be able to perceive things as he _____ them. If you do not do this, you cannot infer accurately the other person's meaning because his percepts may be very _____ from your percepts.
(5-22) evaluate listen understanding	(5-23) Another reason why it is difficult to learn to listen with understanding is that it requires courage. If you enter the perceptual world of somebody else without making evaluations, you run the risk of being changed. Your taking this _____ requires courage.

(3-31) fear	(3-32) The situation that will most likely produce fear in an individual is the perception of danger or some form of _____ and the inability to _____ the situation.
(3-38) anger	(3-39) It is important to remember that an essential feature in the situation producing anger is that the person can identify the _____ to his _____.
(3-45) pride shame	(3-46) The emotion of guilt is different from the emotion of shame. The determinant of shame is an inability to succeed at the desired behavior and as a result, the person sees *himself* as being "_____."
(3-52) destroy	(3-53) The essential situation for the emotion of jealousy is a person's perception of a loved one giving affection to someone else. A person's perception of a "rival" for the affection of a loved one can easily evoke the emotion of _____.

(5-5)	(5-6)
evaluate judge	You may also find yourself making some judgment about me such as, "He doesn't know much about learning," or "He knows a lot about learning." Whatever your judgment, your tendency will be to base your judgment on an _____ made from your frame of reference.
(5-13) perceive perceive	(5-14) The perceptual approach is based upon the viewpoint that the perceiver's behavior is based upon his unique _____ of himself and the world in which he lives and the meaning these _____ have for him.
(5-21) listen understanding	(5-22) Generally, you are not aware of your tendency to _____ the statements of others. This is because it seems to be a natural tendency—you do it without thinking about it. It is not, however, a natural tendency for you to _____ with _____. That is why it is a difficult procedure to learn.

(3-32)	(3-33)
threat avoid	Often, people experience the feeling of fear when they cannot identify the source of their fear. This kind of fear is usually referred to as anxiety. One explanation of the relationship of fear to anxiety is that anxiety is a general state of _____.
(3-39) obstacle goal	(3-40) Fear, joy, and anger are often referred to as the basic or primary emotions and they have in common the fact that they are generally associated with goal-attainment. Goal-attainment is a situational feature of the emotions of _____, _____, and _____. These emotions are often referred to as the basic or _____ emotions.
(3-46) bad	(3-47) A feeling of guilt, however, is evoked by a person's perception of his behavior as being wrong or immoral. It is not associated with inability to attain a goal successfully but with wrongdoing or "_____" behavior. In other words, a person who perceives his behavior as "bad" may experience _____ but a person who sees himself as "bad" will more likely experience _____.
(3-53) jealousy	(3-54) The emotion of envy may be evoked when a person perceives another person as possessing something he wants for himself. He may covet the other person's possessions, success, or some form of perceived superiority. The stronger a person desires something possessed by another the more likely he is to experience the emotion of _____.

(5-4) evaluate judge	(5-5) Let's look at another example. If I say "This programmed approach to learning makes a lot of sense," the chances are that your response will be to _____ the statement and then to _____ it.
(5-12) percepts	(5-13) People behave according to the "facts" as they _____ them. The perceptual approach to understanding the meaning of the other person involves viewing the situation as the other person perceives it to be, not as you _____ the "facts."
(5-20) emotions	(5-21) At this point you may be thinking that you are already a very good listener. It is probably true, however, that your listening has not been the kind we are now talking about. Most people must practice to learn how to _____ with _____.
(5-28) error practice	**END OF SECTION 1** Turn to page 99 and begin Section 2.

(3-33) fear	(3-34) Anxiety, when it is experienced consciously, can best be described as an *objectless* and *pervasive* state of apprehension. A person who feels uneasy but cannot identify the source of his uneasiness may be experiencing anxiety, which is an _____ and _____ state of apprehension.
(3-40) fear joy anger primary	(3-41) Another class of emotions has as its essential determinant a person's perception of his behavior as "good" or "bad" as determined by his standards for behavior. Feelings of guilt, shame, pride, success, and failure can be thus classified since they are evoked by a person's perception of his _____ as being "_____" or "_____."
(3-47) bad guilt shame	(3-48) An essential difference between shame and guilt is that guilt can be experienced as a result of wrongdoing connected with a specific act and not necessarily related to one's perception of oneself as a person as would be the case with the emotion of _____.
(3-54) envy	(3-55) Envy is one of the emotions that has as its situational condition a person's relations with others. Other emotions that share this characteristic are _____, _____, and _____.

(5-3) judging	(5-4) If, after evaluating and judging the other person's statement, you find that you are either agreeing or disagreeing, you are either approving or disapproving the statement. Again, it seems that we have a natural tendency to _____ what is said by the other person and then to _____ the statement.
(5-11) perceptual approach	(5-12) This viewpoint is based on the hypothesis that people do not behave on the basis of how other people see things, but on the basis of their own _____.
(5-19) emotions	(5-20) Listening with understanding is difficult since it is not an easy matter to disregard our own _____ and think only in terms of how the other person may feel.
(5-27) listening understanding	(5-28) When you have overcome the natural tendency to evaluate, to judge, and to approve or disapprove the verbal statements of others, and have learned to listen with understanding instead, you will have overcome one of the important sources of _____ in interpersonal perception. To attain this goal, however, will require a great deal of _____ on your part.

(3-34) objectless pervasive	**(3-35)** Joy is another emotion characterized by a situational condition. Here, the essential determinant is the achievement of a desired goal. A person who attains a goal that he has long strived to attain can be expected to experience the emotion of _____. Return to page 44 for the next item.
(3-41) behavior "bad" "good"	**(3-42)** The feelings of success and failure are determined by a person's perception of the quality of his performance compared with his expectations. If his performance equals or exceeds his expectations, he may experience the feeling of _____. Return to page 44 for the next item.
(3-48) shame	**(3-49)** In many situations, however, when a person fails to live up to his own perception of his ideal self and also violates society's standards for behavior, he may experience a combination of both _____ and _____feelings. Return to page 44 for the next item.
(3-55) love hate jealousy	**END OF SECTION 2** Turn to page 51 and begin Section 3.

(5-2) frame reference	(5-3) After evaluating a statement, you may then judge and approve or disapprove the statement. If, after evaluating the statement, you decide it is true, you are _____ the statement and probably approving.
(5-10) errors	(5-11) Understanding the meaning of the other person on a basis of his perceptions rather than on a basis of how we see things has been referred to as the perceptual approach. When we ignore the perceptions of the other person, we are not using the _____ _____.
(5-18) listening understanding	(5-19) If we are to achieve the other person's frame of reference regarding his statement, we must perceive his needs, motives, and emotions and disregard our own _____ that may be involved.
(5-26) emotions	(5-27) Then, when you can understand the emotions and motives that flavor the other person's statements, you can understand the meaning his statements have for him. This is what we mean by _____ with _____.

Section 3: Identifying Emotions

If you are to identify a person's specific emotions, it becomes necessary for you to infer the specific needs and desires that he is experiencing. The most obvious way of doing this would seem to be simply asking the person to tell what needs and desires he is experiencing at that time. You could then infer his motives and emotions. This approach is fraught with error, however, for several reasons. The person may be experiencing multiple needs that make it difficult to report clearly what he is experiencing. Or he may be unwilling to expose his needs and desires, and simply lie about them. A more basic problem with this approach, however, is that even if the person is willing and reports his needs and desires as he perceives them, his percept may not be accurate. In other words, he may be unaware of his own needs, motives, and emotions and their effects upon his behavior.

Another approach to inferring the motives and emotions of another person is to study his behavior and base your inference on the nature of the behavior. This is the approach that will be employed here, using the person's verbal behavior as a basis for inference.

As you attempt to identify a person's emotions by analyzing his verbal behavior, it is important to remember that human beings do not necessarily experience one need or emotion at a time. Most often a person experiences multiple emotions. For example, the person who feels jealous may also experience feelings of anger at the same time, because some other person is perceived as a barrier to goal-attainment. One form of negative feeling toward another person may also accompany or result from other negative forms of emotion directed toward that person. An example of this would be the feeling of hate for an object of jealousy. The important point to remember is that the range of human emotions is vast and often complex. At best, we make inferences about another person's emotions cautiously with the understanding that our inference must be validated in some manner before we can accept it with certainty.

This section is designed to provide practice in identifying the emotions that were described previously. You have already learned that normal human speech is one of the prominent means of expressing emotions, and both verbal content and vocal mode are important factors. Unfortunately, a printed text cannot convey vocal mode and, therefore, that factor cannot be considered here.

You will find that a new feature has been added in this section. The items that follow call for a choice to be made from several alternatives rather than for supplying missing words in statements. The procedure to be followed, however, is the same as before. As done previously, work rows of frames; after selecting the response that you think is most appropriate, turn the page, and the correct response will be found on the next page along with the next item.

Now turn to page 52 and begin with item 3-56.

(5-1) evaluate	(5-2) You will probably evaluate the statement from your frame of reference rather than from the other person's _____ of _____.
(5-9) error frame reference	(5-10) When you view things from your own frame of reference, i.e., on the basis of your own attitudes and beliefs, you may not infer accurately the meaning of the other person, since his frame of reference, or percepts, may be very different from your frame of reference. Ignoring the other person's frame of reference can lead to serious _____ in your interpersonal perceptions.
(5-17) emotions	(5-18) One way to avoid the tendency to evaluate, judge, or approve or disapprove the statements of others is to "listen with understanding." When you perceive the expressed idea from the other person's perceptual frame of reference, you are said to be "_____ with _____."
(5-25) practice perceptual	(5-26) The best way to learn to listen with understanding is to practice doing it. This means perceiving the meaning of the other person's statement from his frame of reference—his needs, motives, and _____.

BEGIN HERE

Select the statement that *best* indicates the existence of the emotion.

(3-56)

FEAR

A. "It will be his fault if it happens."

B. "It will be my fault if it happens."

C. "I know now that I will be blamed."

D. "I'm being trapped and can't prevent it."

(3-64)

C

A feature of hate is the desire to destroy the hated object or person.

(3-65)

JEALOUSY

A. "He needs the money and must work nights."

B. "I can't stand his mother—all she does is talk."

C. "She has things that I could never afford."

D. "He can't date me often because he's busy with his mother."

BEGIN HERE	**(5-1)** It seems that we have a natural tendency to evaluate what is said by the other person. For example, when someone says, "I think the University is unaware of student needs," your most likely response is to _____ what has been said.
(5-8) evaluate judging judgment	**(5-9)** The tendency to evaluate the statements of others can be viewed as another cause of error in interpersonal perception. The reason it is an important source of _____ is that, when you evaluate statements, you tend to ignore the percepts of the person making the statements and to evaluate them from your _____ of _____.
(5-16) evaluate judge	**(5-17)** It is not an easy matter to avoid the tendency to evaluate. This is particularly true when our own _____ are strongly involved.
(5-24) risk emotions	**(5-25)** Since learning to listen with understanding is difficult, it seems reasonable that it requires a good deal of *practice,* if you are to become proficient at doing it. Learning to listen with understanding requires _____ as well as the courage to risk entering the other person's _____ world.

(3-56)

D

The key to fear is an inability to deal with the threat.

(3-57)

ANXIETY

A. "I feel so tense. I just know that something bad is going to happen."

B. "I hate waiting to take this exam. I know that I'll flunk it."

C. "I just can't stand waiting for my grades."

D. "What if nobody asks me to dance?"

(3-65)

D

Jealousy involves a person's perception of a loved one giving affection to someone else.

(3-66)

ENVY

A. "He worked hard to get the job."

B. "The job was mine until he came along."

C. "She likes him more than she likes me."

D. "He does that job better than I could do it."

UNIT V

THE PERCEPTUAL APPROACH
TO UNDERSTANDING OTHERS

There are a number of approaches to understanding the meaning of others. While these approaches differ in many significant respects, they have in common a concern for the perceptions of the other individual. It would seem that if we are to understand the other person's behavior, we must first understand how he perceives the world around him.

For most of us, it is not an easy matter to enter another person's perceptual world so that we can understand how he is perceiving events and situations. We seem generally to have a natural tendency to evaluate, to judge, and to approve or disapprove the behavior of the other person on a basis of our own needs, motives, and emotions—our own frame of reference. Out attempts at understanding the other person are at best based upon our knowledge of the factors that might influence his perceptions.

There are, then, two ways in which we can attempt to understand the meaning of the other person. One way is by explaining the other person's behavior in terms of our own frame of reference—our perceptions of how things are, and our knowledge of the factors that might influence the other person's perceptions. But we must accept that knowledge of dynamics is not necessarily followed by understanding. The other way, the perceptual approach, is to perceive things in terms of how the other person perceives them—we must attempt to interpret the other's behavior from the other's frame of reference. This is admittedly a difficult task.

Thus, it seems that if we are to make a choice in determining how we go about understanding the meaning, motives, and emotions of others, our choice is between the difficult and the impossible. It is between trying to understand the other person from our frame of reference, which is impossible, and trying to understand him from his own frame of reference, which is difficult. It is difficult because perceiving things as the other person perceives them is not a natural tendency for most of us.

The purpose of this unit is to give you more of an understanding of the problems involved with your entering the perceptual world of others and practice in doing it. Turn to page 91 and begin.

(3-57)

A

Remember, anxiety has been described as an objectless state of apprehension.

(3-58)

JOY

A. "I was certainly surprised."

B. "I really enjoyed the party."

C. "After all these years, I finally made a hole-in-one."

D. "Our team sure was great—winning like that."

(3-66)

B

Envy is a negative feeling that we direct toward another person who possesses something that we covet for ourselves.

(3-67)

FEAR

A. "I know my grades will be bad."

B. "I don't know what's bothering me."

C. "If I failed those tests, I'll be booted out of school."

D. "I have a feeling that I acted wrongly."

16. "I don't care if I ever graduate."

        (a) rationalization   (d) projection

        (b) compensation   (e) reaction-formation

        (c) identification   (f) none of these

17. "I just do not want to accept their values."

        (a) rationalization   (d) projection

        (b) compensation   (e) reaction-formation

        (c) identification   (f) none of these

18. "My only interest is to be the best teacher ever."

        (a) rationalization   (d) projection

        (b) compensation   (e) reaction-formation

        (c) identification   (f) none of these

19. "I can't get my work done because of all the noise in the dorm."

        (a) rationalization   (d) projection

        (b) compensation   (e) reaction-formation

        (c) identification   (f) none of these

20. "Religion has never been a concern for me."

        (a) rationalization   (d) projection

        (b) compensation   (e) reaction-formation

        (c) identification   (f) none of these

(3-58)	(3-59)
C	**ANGER**
The essential situational condition for joy is striving toward a goal and attaining it. Generally, the longer the striving, the greater is the joy.	A. "I just don't seem able to do it." B. "I can't stand being around him." C. "I'd have won if it hadn't been for him getting in my way." D. "It seems like the harder I try to win the worse I do."

(3-67)	(3-68)
C	**ANGER**
The grades are perceived as threatening and there is an inability to change the outcome.	A. "My job is twice as difficult because of him." B. "I've tried six times and still can't do it." C. "Next time I'll try harder." D. "I'm just tired of trying."

The following statements can be viewed as examples of rationalization, compensation, identification, projection, reaction-formation, or none of these defense mechanisms. View these statements on this basis and select the response that describes the statement best.

10. "The only reason that I cheat on exams is that everybody else does it."

    (a) rationalization   (d) projection

    (b) compensation   (e) reaction-formation

    (c) identification   (f) none of these

11. "Everybody is out to get the best of you."

    (a) rationalization   (d) projection

    (b) compensation   (e) reaction-formation

    (c) identification   (f) none of these

12. "I think I might get along better with other people if I would try harder."

    (a) rationalization   (d) projection

    (b) compensation   (e) reaction-formation

    (c) identification   (f) none of these

13. "It's only money. Money isn't important to me."

    (a) rationalization   (d) projection

    (b) compensation   (e) reaction-formation

    (c) identification   (f) none of these

14. "All people have a problem with their sexual behavior."

    (a) rationalization   (d) projection

    (b) compensation   (e) reaction-formation

    (c) identification   (f) none of these

15. "My college has higher standards than any of those eastern colleges."

    (a) rationalization   (d) projection

    (b) compensation   (e) reaction-formation

    (c) identification   (f) none of these

(3-59)

C

Anger is most likely to occur when the obstacle to goal-attainment is known.

(3-60)

PRIDE

A. "I'm doing the kind of job now that I should do."

B. "I won, but it wasn't my best game."

C. "I'm capable of doing even better."

D. "I'm just glad that I played well enough to win."

(3-68)

A

Being able to identify the barrier to goal-attainment makes anger more likely to occur.

(3-69)

SHAME

A. "That was a bad thing to do."

B. "It's not like me to do something so wrong."

C. "Everybody knows the right thing to do."

D. "I should have worked it differently."

Proficiency Test for Unit IV

Again, missing words should be supplied in the spaces provided for these test questions. Then, after you have answered all the questions, check your answers with those in the answer key at the rear of the text. Do not forget to review the material in the text where your test answers indicate this is necessary.

Supply the missing words in the following statements.

1. Anxiety is always an _____ emotional experience.

2. The source of anxiety may be _____ and not known to the person who is experiencing it.

3. Anxiety may be controlled and kept at a low level by either _____ responses or _____ responses.

4. Defense mechanisms is another term used for referring to _____ responses.

5. The defense mechanism used to ascribe an acceptable motive to behavior which is motivated by needs that past training has made to appear unacceptable is referred to as _____.

6. Reaction-formation involves an individual behaving in a manner _____ to that which is dictated unconsciously.

7. A person who ascribes the qualities and traits of another person or object to himself is employing a defense mechanism referred to as

_____.

8. A defense mechanism that can be considered the opposite of identification is _____.

9. When a person is unable to achieve direct satisfaction of a motive and, in order to allay the resulting frustration and anxiety, accepts a substitute goal or activity that gives partial satisfaction, he is said to be employing _____ as a defense mechanism.

(3-60)	(3-61)
A	**SHAME**
Pride is the result of seeing your behavior as being in accord with your ideal self.	A. "Everybody thinks I didn't do well." B. "It's ridiculous that I could have failed such a simple test." C. "My mother thinks I didn't do well." D. "I didn't study and I failed."
(3-69)	(3-70)
B	**GUILT**
Shame involves a person's perception of his ideal self.	A. "I'm not really that kind of person." B. "It's not like me to do something that is so wrong." C. "I'm capable of doing better." D. "I don't know why I did it. I knew it was wrong."

(4-59)	(4-60)
B	A. "I like to read pornography." B. "I am absolutely horrified by the lewd, pornographic material on magazine racks." C. "I wonder how they get around the law with that stuff." D. "I guess people want that kind of material or else it wouldn't be displayed there." Return to page 84 for the next item.
(4-62)	(4-63)
C	A. "I have never ever given the slightest thought to it. That is beneath me." B. "Sometimes at night I think about it." C. "Everybody else thinks about it. Why shouldn't I?" D. "Well, maybe I have thought about it once or twice." Return to page 84 for the next item.

(3-61)

B

Shame results from perceiving your behavior as falling short of *your* ideal self—not somebody else's standard.

(3-62)

GUILT

A. "Stealing is bad and I should not have done it."

B. "I should have known that I'd get caught."

C. "I'm capable of doing much better."

D. "It depends on what you steal."

(3-70)

D

Guilt differs from shame. With feelings of guilt, the emphasis is on "bad" or "immoral" behavior.

(3-71)

HATE

A. "When she's around, I leave."

B. "She's the cause of all my trouble."

C. "I want to like her, but there is something about her that turns me off."

D. "When I finish with her, she won't even have a job or be able to get one."

(4-58)	(4-59)
(no response required)	A. "Most times, I feel I have love for my fel-low-men."
	B. "I feel nothing but love for my fellow-men. How could anyone feel differently?"
	C. "I try to love my fellow-men, but have a difficult time doing it."
	D. "At times, I don't think I love anyone."

(4-61)	(4-62)
	A. "I can't really understand homosexuality."
	B. "You just have to accept that some people are that way."
B	C. "It is absolutely repulsive even to think of it. I could never do such a thing."
	D. "Maybe it's worth a try."

(4-64)	
	### END OF UNIT IV
D	Turn to page 87 now for a test to determine how well you understand the material present-ed in Unit IV.

(3-62)

A

Guilt is a feeling of having done a "bad" or "wrong" deed.

(3-63)

LOVE

A. "I enjoy being with her."

B. "She gives me everything that I want."

C. "When I'm with her, it's different."

D. "I want to be with her forever."

(3-71)

D

Again, there is the desire to destroy the hated person. Here dislike would probably only lead to avoidance of the disliked person.

(3-72)

ENVY

A. "Why should he have more than I have?"

B. "He sure is conceited."

C. "He stole my girl away from me."

D. "I can't stand him."

BEGIN HERE *Reaction-formation*	**(4-58)** This defense mechanism involves preventing dangerous desires from being expressed by *exaggerating* opposed attitudes. In reaction-formation there may be a tendency for the person to make frequent protestations of his feelings. Identify the statements in the following items that serve as the best examples of reaction-formation. (no response required)
(4-60) B	**(4-61)** A. "Sometimes I feel frightened when aggressive people confront me." B. "I never feel frightened when aggressive people confront me." C. "Everybody is hostile." D. "Sometimes I do and sometimes I don't."
(4-63) A	**(4-64)** A. "I lie only when it helps my cause." B. "Everybody lies sometime." C. "To tell a lie is to commit a sin." D. "I would never tell a lie."

(3-63)

D

An essential feature of all forms of love is its enduring quality.

(3-64)

HATE

A. "He cheated."

B. "I dislike him intensely."

C. "I wish he were dead."

D. "I hardly know him, but I can't stand him."

Return to page 52 for the next item.

(3-72)

A

Envy never seems to be expressed directly. It's difficult for most people to admit to a feeling of envy even when they recognize it.

END OF UNIT III

Turn to page 61 for the proficiency test for Unit III.

(4-52)	(4-53)
B	A. "Some money is missing from my room."
	B. "Things have been missing in the past."
	C. "With so many people around, you can be sure that somebody will have sticky fingers."
	D. "Under these circumstances, it might be wise to lock the door."
	Return to page 81 for the next item.
(4-55)	(4-56)
D	A. "Some people think only of themselves."
	B. "I don't always think of others first."
	C. "Everybody thinks of number one first."
	D. "Why should we think of others?"
	Return to page 81 for the next item.

Proficiency Test for Unit III

The purpose of this proficiency test is to give you an opportunity to test your understanding of the concepts of needs, motives, and emotions and to test your ability to identify the possible existence of specific emotions by interpreting verbal statements. Again, when you have completed the test, return to the text for clarification of any test items that give you difficulty before proceeding to Unit IV.

Supply the missing words in the following statements.

1. It is possible to categorize needs as _____ and _____.

2. The individual's subjective feelings of pleasantness and unpleasantness are usually referred to as _____ by psychologists.

3. It is probably fair to say that human beings are always in some state of _____ which produces internal drive states.

4. The human's needs, motives, and emotions are intimately _____.

5. Emotions can be identified in others by observing and interpreting expressive reactions such as facial changes and other bodily reactions. You can also identify the possible existence of emotions in others by interpreting their _____ behavior.

6. The instigation of behavior that is associated with internal responses produced by needs has been referred to by psychologists as _____.

7. A person who perceives the quality of his performance as falling short of his ideal self-image may see *himself* as being "bad" and, as a result, may experience the emotion of _____.

8. When an individual is blocked in his efforts toward goal-attainment and can identify the person or object that is blocking him, the emotion of _____ may result.

(4-51)	(4-52)
(no response required)	A. "I think about sex often."
	B. "All that anyone in that dorm ever thinks about is sex."
	C. "Sex is a popular topic of conversation in the dorm."
	D. "I don't like to talk about sex."

(4-54)	(4-55)
	A. "There may be some cheating in that class."
	B. "I am afraid that I might try to cheat if given the chance."
A	C. "I have seen some cheating in that class."
	D. "Everyone is trying to cheat in one way or another."

(4-57)	
	END OF SECTION 5
A or D Both are projections	Turn to page 84 and begin Section 6.

9. Three emotional experiences that usually have goal-attainment as a situational characteristic are _____, _____, and ____.

10. The emotion usually associated with the attainment of a desired goal is

____.

11. The emotions that are determined by a person's perception of the quality of his performance compared with his expectations are _____ and

_____.

12. Four emotions that have as their situational determinant a person's relations with others are _____, _____, _____, and _____.

The following verbal expressions may indicate the existence of emotions for the individuals making the statement. In the space provided, indicate the emotion you think most probably exists.

13. _____ "I don't know why I feel so uneasy."

14. _____ "If I flunk this test, I'm in trouble."

15. _____ "It may be right, but I should have done better."

16. _____ "My mother tells me she doesn't care for him but when he is home she spends all of her time with him."

17. _____ "I would just like to get rid of her."

18. _____ "If the author had done a better job with this text, I could learn this stuff."

19. _____ "I knew it was wrong when I did it. I feel just terrible."

20. _____ "I feel drawn to him—I can't help myself."

21. _____ "I'm pleased with myself. I feel I did a good job."

22. _____ "It's beneath me to behave as badly as I did."

BEGIN HERE *Projection*	**(4-51)** Projection is a defense mechanism by which an individual attributes to others his own undesirable, unconscious feelings and motives. Generally, this involves placing blame for difficulties upon others or attributing one's own unethical desires to others. Select the statement in each of the following items that serves as the best example of projection. (no response required)
(4-53) C	**(4-54)** A. "I am always friendly, but everyone else is so hostile." B. "I do something that makes people react to me with a great deal of hostility at times." C. "I prefer to be by myself." D. "Some people just don't seem to like me."
(4-56) C	**(4-57)** A. "I take the same deductions that everyone else takes." B. "I take every deduction I can." C. "I really don't cheat on my taxes." D. "Everybody cheats a little on income tax."

UNIT IV

IDENTIFYING HIDDEN MEANING

Until now we have been concerned with identifying emotions that the other person is aware of and perhaps even trying to communicate to you; their existence and origins are known to him, and he is making no deliberate effort to hide or disguise the emotions. But what about the person who is "laughing on the outside and crying on the inside"? If we are to perceive accurately the meaning of the other person, we cannot depend on only those emotions that he is able and willing to communicate by means of bodily reactions and verbalizations. Those emotions that are hidden, consciously or unconsciously, by the other person also need to be interpreted if we are to perceive him accurately.

The purpose of this unit is to provide a basis for identifying hidden emotions. Anxiety in particular will be emphasized in order to improve your ability to identify latent anxiety.

Obviously, you will be aware of and easily identify uncontrolled anxiety manifesting itself in overt behavior such as nervousness. It is not, however, an easy task for you to be aware of anxiety in others when they keep that anxiety at a low level by means of responses that do not exhibit themselves in obvious ways.

Upon completing this unit of study, you should have a competency in recognizing controlled anxiety in others by interpreting certain kinds of symptomatic verbalizations.

Turn to page 64 and begin with Section 1. You should continue to work rows of frames across pages as you have done in previous units.

(4-45)	(4-46)
A	A. "My dog really was courageous even though he was only half the size of the other dog." B. "My dog held his own." C. "I didn't think my dog would get out of it alive." D. "My dog got in a fight and lost." Return to page 78 for the next item.
(4-48)	(4-49)
D	A. "He has a great way of dealing with people." B. "I deal with people the same way he does." C. "I would like to have his talent for dealing with people." D. "I just don't seem to have the touch that he has." Return to page 78 for the next item.

BEGIN HERE	**(4-1)** According to one rationale, anxiety can be regarded as an unpleasant emotional experience related to fear. The feeling that results when people experience the emotion of fear but cannot identify the source of their fear has been referred to as _____. This is an _____ emotional experience.
(4-8) instrumental	**(4-9)** Noninstrumental responses reduce anxiety without resulting in any change in the causative conflict or frustration by operating to deny, falsify, or distort reality. Denying that an anxiety-producing situation actually exists may _____ anxiety and the _____ feeling it produces.
(4-16) latent	**(4-17)** In this program, we will be concerned mostly with the defense mechanisms that people use to reduce and control anxiety. You should recall that these mechanisms act to _____, _____, or _____ reality.
(4-24) rejection	**(4-25)** Projection and identification are alike in that they both may occur when a person perceives himself as having undesirable characteristics and anxiety is aroused. When the self-perception does not include traits that the individual desires, _____ may occur. When the self-perception includes traits that the individual does not desire, _____ may occur.

(4-44)	(4-45)
(no response required)	A. "I get angry when I hear them saying things like that about the President. He's not like that."
	B. "People should not talk about other people when they don't even know them."
	C. "I don't pay much attention to that kind of talk."
	D. "Maybe what they say is true."
(4-47)	(4-48)
	A. "I like Helen a great deal."
	B. "I like Helen a great deal and admire her."
	C. "Helen is more popular than I am."
D	D. "I have a lot of Helen's characteristics. We are really very much alike."
(4-50)	
	END OF SECTION 4
C	Turn to page 81 and begin Section 5.

(4-1)	(4-2)
anxiety unpleasant	Anxiety is an upsetting state. It can be regarded as an unpleasant emotional experience. When anxiety is experienced consciously, it can best be described as an objectless and pervasive state of apprehension. A person who feels uneasy, but cannot identify the source of his uneasiness, may be experiencing _____.
(4-9) reduce unpleasant	(4-10) Responses that operate to deny, falsify, or distort reality are referred to as _____ responses.
(4-17) deny falsify distort	(4-18) Theorists have postulated a number of defense mechanisms that people use to reduce _____. The reduction of anxiety is a function of _____ _____.
(4-25) identification projection	(4-26) Reaction-formation is another of the defense mechanisms. Reaction-formation occurs when the individual behaves in a manner *opposite* to what is dictated by his unconscious feelings. The stingy person who unconsciously believes that stinginess is bad and a cause of rejection by others and reacts by spending freely and acting as if he didn't care is using _____ to control the anxiety caused by the threat of doing a bad thing and being rejected.

BEGIN HERE *Identification*	**(4-44)** Identification refers to the ascribing to one's self of qualities and characteristics belonging actually to another person or object. Identify the statement in each of the following items that best indicates that the person making the statement may be identifying in some manner. (no response required)
(4-46) A	**(4-47)** A. "I like to keep my car in good shape." B. "I like to race other cars from stop signs." C. "My car needs a new paint job." D. "My car is really powerful. There are not many that could keep up with it."
(4-49) B	**(4-50)** A. "He really does an excellent job." B. "I wish I had his ability." C. "I would run things very much as he does." D. "He makes inexcusable mistakes."

(4-2) anxiety	(4-3) The actual source of anxiety is very often uncon-scious and not known to the person who is experienc-ing it. While the _____ of anxiety may not be known to the person who is experiencing it, the per-son is always aware of the _____ feeling that is present.
(4-10) noninstrumental	(4-11) Noninstrumental responses are also referred to as de-fense mechanisms. These mechanisms operate in such a way as to deny, falsify, or _____ reality so that anxiety may be reduced.
(4-18) anxiety defense mechanisms	(4-19) Rationalization is one such mechanism. Rationaliza-tion refers to ascribing an acceptable motive to be-havior that is motivated by needs that past training has made to appear unacceptable. An individual may use _____ to distort reality so as to control anxiety.
(4-26) reaction- formation	(4-27) By using reaction-formation, a person protects him-self from acknowledging that he possesses feelings and motives that are *unacceptable* to him. He distorts reality so as to be able to see his feelings and motives as the _____ of what they really are.

(4-38)	(4-39)
	A. "I like to dance."
	B "My idea of a nice evening is a dinner date and then dancing."
D	C. "I am really a very good dancer and would rather dance than anything I can think of."
	D. "I like to dance a lot."
	Return to page 75 for the next item.
(4-41)	(4-42)
	A. "I like to play bridge a great deal."
	B. "I would rather play bridge than do anything else."
C	C. "Bridge is certainly fun. I enjoy spending an evening playing bridge."
	D. "I dislike bridge."
	Return to page 75 for the next item.

(4-3) source unpleasant	(4-4) The source of anxiety may often be unknown but the emotional state of anxiety and the unpleasant feeling that it produces is a _____ state.
(4-11) distort	(4-12) Noninstrumental responses, or _____ mechanisms, operate for most people to keep anxiety at a low level. They do this by operating to _____, falsify, or distort reality.
(4-19) rationalization	(4-20) Another defense mechanism is that of compensation. When a person is unable to achieve direct satisfaction of a motive and, in order to allay frustration and anxiety, he accepts a substitute goal or activity that gives partial satisfaction, he is said to be using compensation. The use of compensation may reduce _____.
(4-27) opposite	(4-28) Just as with identification and projection, reaction-formation may result when an individual possesses feelings and motives that are _____ to him.

(4-37)

(no response required)

(4-38)

A. "I just play for the fun."

B. "It's tough losing after you have spent a lot of time practicing."

C. "I like golf. I'll try again next year."

D. "I spend every spare minute I have on the golf course."

(4-40)

A

(4-41)

A. "I guess I don't have time for it and should give it up."

B. "I guess I don't have time for it, but I feel they need me."

C. "Even though it takes up all of my time, I could never leave my group."

D. "I'll stay as long as I feel it's profitable."

(4-43)

D

END OF SECTION 3

Turn to page 78 and begin Section 4.

(4-4) conscious (or known)	(4-5) In other words, anxiety is always a _____ state even though its source is very likely to be _____ to the person who is experiencing it.
(4-12) defense deny	(4-13) Defense mechanisms fail occasionally to keep anxiety at a low level, however, and at those times anxiety is felt in full force. This uncontrolled anxiety manifests itself in overt behavior such as nervousness, which is observed easily by others. When defense mechanisms fail, it is because they did not operate successfully to _____, _____, or _____ reality.
(4-20) anxiety	(4-21) Identification is a defense mechanism signifying the ascription to one's self of qualities and characteristics belonging to another person or object. A person who acts as if he shared in the traits or prestige of another person is said to be _____ with that person.
(4-28) unacceptable	(4-29) In other words, identification, projection, and reaction-formation are all used to distort self-perceptions that are seen as _____ by the individual and if acknowledged consciously would produce a state of _____.

	(4-37)
BEGIN HERE	Compensation is a mechanism by which a person accepts a substitute goal or behavior that he perceives as being attainable or socially acceptable in place of a desired goal or activity that he feels is unacceptable or unattainable. A characteristic of compensation is that the behavior seems obviously exaggerated. Select the statement in each of the following items that indicates compensation. (no response required)
Compensation	

(4-39)	(4-40)
	A. "Even though I date a lot, I don't want to get too involved with anybody. I date a different girl every time."
	B. "I enjoy having close relationships."
C	C. "I'll probably get married some day, but not now."
	D. "I try to have at least two dates every week."

(4-42)	(4-43)
	A. "My work is very demanding."
	B. "I don't like my work, but I do it."
	C. "I spend what time I must at my work."
B	D. "I spend all my time working."

(4-5) conscious unknown	(4-6) Since anxiety is an unpleasant emotional experience, the human organism naturally attempts to reduce it and produce a more pleasant state. In other words, it seems that the organism naturally attempts to reduce _____ .
(4-13) deny falsify distort	(4-14) These observable effects of anxiety, which occur when defense mechanisms fail to operate efficiently, are the reason we refer to anxiety that is controlled as latent anxiety. In other words, when defense mechanisms operate to control anxiety, we refer to the state of anxiety as _____ .
(4-21) identifying	(4-22) Another form of identification is demonstrated when a person reacts to objects, usually those he possesses, as if they were parts of himself and as if he shared in the characteristics of the object. A person who acts proud because his automobile is very powerful may be perceiving himself as possessing such power. In such a case, the person is _____ with the power of his car.
(4-29) unacceptable anxiety	END OF SECTION 1 Go to page 71, turn the page over, and you will see page 72, upside-down. Turn the book around and begin Section 2 on page 72.

(4-31)	(4-32)
B	A. "I don't plan to go out because I'm not asked out very often." B. "I feel miserable because I'm not asked out." C. "I really don't mind not having dates because I would rather study." D. "Some girls always seem to have dates." Return to page 72 for the next item.
(4-34)	(4-35)
B	A. "I try, but she still treats me badly." B. "I guess I just don't try hard enough." C. "I could try harder, but it would take a lot of effort." D. "I don't even try because it wouldn't do any good." Return to page 72 for the next item.

(4-6) anxiety	(4-7) The responses that individuals acquire to reduce anxiety can be classified as instrumental responses and noninstrumental responses. An individual may be able to reduce or control anxiety with either _____ responses or with _____ responses.
(4-14) latent	(4-15) While uncontrolled anxiety manifests itself in overt behavior and is easily recognized, latent anxiety does not have this characteristic. Therefore, it is more difficult to recognize a state of _____ anxiety.
(4-22) identifying	(4-23) Projection is a defense mechanism by which an individual ascribes to others his own feelings and motives that he believes to be undesirable. In a sense, projection can be considered as the opposite of identification and identification can be considered as the opposite of _____.

(4-30)	(4-31)
(no response required)	A. "The more I study, the better I do on tests." B. "The more I study, the worse I do on tests." C. "I'm lazy and should study more." D. "I don't like to study."
(4-33) C	(4-34) A. "Premarital sexual relations may cause serious consequences." B. "I love Jim and for that reason I think sexual relations are O.K." C. "I try to be careful so that nothing will go wrong." D. "I guess it's bad, but I do it anyway."
(4-36) C	END OF SECTION 2 Turn to page 75 and begin Section 3.

(4-7) instrumental noninstrumental	(4-8) Instrumental responses reduce anxiety by the elimination of the causative conflict or frustration. As an example, a person who leaves a movie because it is causing a feeling of anxiety for him is using an _____ response to eliminate the cause of his anxiety. Return to page 64 for the next item.
(4-15) latent	(4-16) When responses to signals of danger are well learned by an individual, he can usually keep the level of anxiety quite low. This kind of anxiety is called _____ anxiety. Return to page 64 for the next item.
(4-23) projection	(4-24) When an individual's self-perception includes traits and characteristics that he does not see as being desirable, he may either identify with another person who is perceived as having the desired characteristics, or he may ascribe his own undesired characteristics to others. The latter behavior is the use of _____ as a defense mechanism. Return to page 64 for the next item.

	(4-30)
BEGIN HERE	Rationalization has been described as a defense mechanism by which a person gives good-sounding, convincing reasons for behavior that is actually motivated by unconscious, socially unacceptable impulses. On the pages that follow, select the statement in each item that best indicates the possible use of rationalization.
Rationalization	(no response required)

(4-32)	(4-33)
	A. "The coach said I'd make the team if I would practice every day."
	B. "Football is just a little too tough for me."
C	C. "I wouldn't make the team because the coach doesn't like me."
	D. "I might make the team if I had time to practice every day."

(4-35)	(4-36)
	A. "I don't know why I did it."
	B. "I did it because somehow I can't say 'no' to anyone."
D	C. "I only did it because I didn't want to hurt his feelings."
	D. "I know I didn't have to do it."

Answer Key
Proficiency Test for Unit I

1. information / environment
2. process / learning / thinking
3. internal
4. implicit personality theory
5. selective
6. "set" / motives
7. self-analysis
8. response
9. inferred
10. learning experiences / thinking
11. interpersonal
12. accuracy

Answer Key
Proficiency Test for Unit II

1. stereotyping / trait attribution / assumed similarity
2. related / trait attribution
3. self-analysis
4. implicit personality theory
5. distortion / intelligence / implicit personality theory
6. assumed similarity
7. stereotyping
8. distortion
9. intelligence
10. implicit personality theory

Answer Key
Proficiency Test for Unit III

1. biological / learned
2. emotions
3. need
4. related
5. verbal
6. motivation
7. shame
8. anger
9. fear / anger / joy
10. joy
11. success / failure
12. love / hate / envy / jealousy
13. anxiety
14. fear
15. shame
16. jealousy
17. hate
18. anger
19. guilt
20. love
21. pride
22. shame

Answer Key
Proficiency Test for Unit IV

1. unpleasant
2. unconscious
3. instrumental / noninstrumental
4. noninstrumental
5. rationalization
6. opposite
7. identification
8. projection
9. compensation
10. a
11. d
12. f
13. e
14. d
15. c
16. e
17. f
18. b
19. a
20. e

Answer Key
Proficiency Test for Unit V

1. perceptual approach
2. evaluate / frame / reference
3. judgment
4. emotions
5. listening / understanding / practice
6. b
7. c
8. a
9. b
10. c
11. b

Answer Key
Final Proficiency Test

1. personality
2. past (or previous) learning / thinking / set / motives
3. interpersonal perception
4. internal
5. verbal
6. error
7. intelligence / distortion / implicit personality theory
8. stereotyping
9. verbal content / affective intent
10. perceptual / frame / reference
11. evaluate
12. self-analysis
13. stereotyping / similarity / trait
14. affective
15. distortion
16. listening / understanding
17. selective
18. implicit personality theory
19. assumed
20. need
21. unpleasant
22. evaluating / emotions
23. latent
24. defense mechanisms
25. instrumental
26. emotions / motives
27. rationalization
28. compensating
29. projecting
30. reaction-formation
31. identification
32. projection
33. compensation
34. none
35. reaction-formation
36. identification
37. rationalization
38. d
39. a
40. c